FARRAR
STRAUS
GIROUX

Isaac B. Singer

Isaac B. Singer

A LIFE

Florence Noiville

Translated from the French by Catherine Temerson

FARRAR, STRAUS AND GIROUX

NEW YORK

Farrar, Straus and Giroux
19 Union Square West, New York 10003

Copyright © 2003 by Éditions Stock
Translation copyright © 2006 by Catherine Temerson
All rights reserved
Distributed in Canada by Douglas & McIntyre Ltd.
Printed in the United States of America
Originally published in 2003 by Éditions Stock, France
Published in the United States by Farrar, Straus and Giroux
First American edition, 2006

Library of Congress Cataloging-in-Publication Data
Noiville, Florence.
    [Isaac B. Singer. English]
    Isaac B. Singer : a life / Florence Noiville ; translated from the French by
Catherine Temerson.— 1st American ed.
        p.   cm.
    Includes bibliographical references.
    ISBN-13: 978-0-374-17800-0 (hardcover : alk. paper)
    ISBN-10: 0-374-17800-3 (hardcover : alk. paper)
    1. Singer, Isaac Bashevis, 1904–1991.   2. Authors, Yiddish—Biography.
I. Title.

PJ5129.S49Z8313 2006
839′.133—dc22

                                                        2006000061

Designed by Jonathan D. Lippincott

www.fsgbooks.com

1   3   5   7   9   10   8   6   4   2

To R., M., and J. Hirsch

Of laughter I said it is madness and of mirth what doeth it?
—Ecclesiastes

Contents

Preface

Isaac Bashevis Singer hated biographies. He said, "When you are really hungry, you don't look for the biography of the baker." He was probably sincere when he added that even if Tolstoy, whom he greatly admired, had lived across the street, he wouldn't have tried to meet him. "The work is what counts, not the man."[1]

Reconstructing the first thirty years of Singer's life in Poland is a difficult task. Everything has been destroyed, burned, swallowed up by the Nazi inferno. Nevertheless, I retraced his steps. I went to Leoncin, on the Vistula, and to Radzymin, his childhood village. I tracked down several of his now elderly contemporaries who had known him in Warsaw. I interviewed his son, who now lives near Tel Aviv and who was five years old when Singer left him behind in Poland. I explored the Singer archives in Texas. In New York, I persuaded Dvorah Telushkin, one of the last women who played a significant role in his life, to meet with me, though she no longer wants to talk about Isaac because she feels his image has been too "tarnished."

Gradually, from behind an ironic, mocking façade, a proud man emerged, possessed of a sobermindedness that should challenge all who perceive him merely as an amiable storyteller or mischievous fabulist of the Jewish soul. In his life and works, one discovers the opposite: a supreme master in the telling of physical and metaphysical distress, one of the modern virtuosos of anguish, inhibition, and fiasco.

Irritating, engaging, and fascinating, this Singer is very different from the widely disseminated stereotypes of his character.

May he forgive this biography, which is not a scholarly work, but *one* interpretation of his life. This book may defy his notion of writers and literature, but, after all, he, too, was familiar with the pleasures of transgression.

Florence Noiville
Paris, June 2003

Isaac B. Singer

ONE

"A Stronghold of Jewish Puritanism"

THE LOCKET-SIZE PHOTO dates from 1926; it is one of the oldest known photographs of Isaac Bashevis Singer. Isaac is twenty-two years old, and he still has some hair, though he won't for very long. He is a thin, fair-skinned redhead whose ears stick way out. The expression in his eyes is beguiling, almost bewitching. His pale, transparent blue eyes seem to gaze inward. One can almost imagine the four-year-old boy who was taught to read with the Pentateuch and almost recognize the face of the future Nobel Prize winner. Incredulity, bafflement: the gaze is simultaneously straightforward and helpless. It is the gaze of a tormented dreamer, a gaze Singer retained all his life, as if his father's words on the Kabbalah still echoed in his ears: "It is not a simple matter, not simple at all. The world is filled with mysteries, everything happens according to its decree, everything contains the secret of secrets . . ."[1]

This photo is strangely symbolic. It dates from the same period when Singer published his first writings. Everything prior to that time—childhood scenes, family albums—has disappeared. We will never know what Isaac looked like as a little boy or as an adolescent. The first time we see his face it is already the face of a younger writer, as if everything that came before—life without fiction—was not worth disclosing. As if he wanted to tell us that his true personality was inseparable from the works behind which he so often hid. The war spared that particular photo by chance, but Singer never believed in chance. The fact that his face is revealed to us for the first time just as he was emerging as a writer is a fitting place to begin his story.

The opening sentence could be Alfred Jarry's grim statement about *Ubu Roi*: "The action takes place in Poland, that is to say, nowhere." This is true even in geographical terms, for, at the beginning of the twentieth century, Poland was divided and under the iron rule of three empires, Russia, Prussia, and Austria. "Nowhere" could be used to describe Singer's native village, too, for today, more than a hundred years after his birth, every last trace of Jewish life has been meticulously obliterated from the landscape. The Poland of Singer's birth is nowhere in human memory. All the eyewitnesses to his 1904 birth have died. If they were still alive today, they would be 110 or 115 years old, assuming they had managed to flee Poland before the Second World War or were among the roughly 120,000 Jews—of the country's original population of three million prior to 1939—who survived the Holocaust.[2]

The only way, then, to reconstruct Isaac's first years is to trust his own recollections. Fortunately, these were unusually precocious and vivid. Isaac always claimed to remember events that had taken place when he was three or even two and a half years old. One day when he referred to his native village of Leoncin, by the sandy banks of the Vistula near Nowy Dwór, his mother was amazed. Isaac was only four years old when the Singer family had left Leoncin. How could he possibly remember anything? Singer described the inhabitants and the houses with such a wealth of detail that she was rendered speechless. He could even recall the villagers' names. His mother couldn't believe her ears. The boy was a prodigy. She didn't know that this ability to remember would inform his entire life, that he would constantly relive, polish, and transform his recollections, and that when his memory betrayed him, he would die.

Yet these extraordinary memories are accompanied by strange areas of darkness, starting with his date of birth. Was Singer born on July 14, 1904, as he often claimed? This is far from certain. He seems to have made up the date. For a novelist to start his life with a fiction is very fitting. Here is how he explained it later: "At our house, we never celebrated birthdays. One day, at the heder, a little schoolmate said to me, 'Today's my birthday, I'm going to receive gifts.' I went home and, furious, asked my mother, 'What about me, when is my birthday? Why don't we ever celebrate it?' Sensing how upset I was, to make me happy my mother answered, 'Well, as a matter of fact, it's today.' The day was July 14, obviously not the real date, but I decided that would be it from then on."[3]

We will probably never know the real date. In Poland, all the relevant archives have disappeared. Singer's birth certificate is nowhere to be found. Was it destroyed during the First World War, or was it burned during the Second World War? Very few official registries of the Jewish communities remain. After 1945, some were found in the midst of ruins or buried in heaps of rubbish. Occasionally, villagers brought the schoolteacher papers covered with writing they couldn't decipher. More often, these documents were used as wrapping paper. In the countryside, herring was wrapped in the Torah.

A trip to Singer's birthplace today is hardly more fruitful. You cross fragrant mossy pine forests and fields still harvested with scythes before reaching Leoncin, about twenty miles northwest of Warsaw. The village stretches along a drab main road, the Street of the Partisans. Not a trace of its former Jewish life remains. The only people you encounter are children and a few men on bicycles with bottles of beer sticking out of their pockets. Today the house where Singer was born is gone; all that remains is an orchard. Across from the town hall, though, a dead-end alley bears the name of Isaac Bashevis Singer. But the graffiti—two stars of David—render the street sign almost illegible. Clearly, Leoncin's inhabitants have no particular desire to honor the great man's memory. No one talks about him; no one remembers him; the silence is deafening. The proposal that the village school be named after him was ignored. Isaac Bashevis Singer Street boasts not a single house; the inhabitants of Leoncin all refused to have a "Jewish address."[4]

A FAMILY OF RABBIS AND WRITERS

Since there are no independent sources, the best way to imagine the setting of those early years is through the autobiographical writings of the Singer children. In the Singer family—as in the Corneille and Brontë families—all the brothers and sisters were writers, or at least attracted to writing. Both Isaac's older brother, Israel Joshua, and his sister, Hinde Esther, recorded their memories of that vanished world. In *Of a World That Is No More*, Israel Joshua describes the shtetl's wooden houses, its sandy roads, the figurine of Puss-in-Boots in the tobacconist's shop window.[5] These recollections are supplemented by those of Hinde Esther, who later became Esther Kreitman, in her memoir *The Dance of Demons*.[6] At the time, Leoncin had a population of two hundred, Jews and non-Jews, who all lived in great poverty but sent their children to the same school and seemed to have coexisted peacefully.

By the time the third child was born, Isaac—Yitskhok, in Yiddish, or Itshele, in the affectionate diminutive—the Singer family had been living in Poland for generations. Four hundred years earlier, in the sixteenth century, that land had become, as the historian Pierre Chanu calls it, the "Far West (in the East) for mistreated Jews . . . For Ashkenazi Jews, the center of gravity moved a thousand kilometers to the East, from the Rhine valley to the Jerusalem on the Polish and Lithuanian borders."[7] The family names still bear the traces of this massive resettlement. Many Polish Jews kept their German names, such as Singer, which means "cantor."

Isaac was born into an extremely pious family. His father, Pinchos Menahem Singer, was a rabbi. So was his grandfather, his father's father, Reb Samuel, and Reb Samuel's father, Reb Isaiah; Reb Isaiah's father had been Reb Moshe, known as the "Sage of Warsaw," and Reb Moshe's father had been Reb Tobias, whose father's name had also been Reb Moshe, and so on, back to a certain Reb Zvi Hirsch. In other words, the men in the Singer family had been rabbis for at least seven generations. Pinchos Menahem's disappointment later on at Isaac's preference for sacrilegious writing over the Talmud and the Torah goes without saying. And, in a country where the general rule was that sons followed in their father's footsteps, so does the determination the young Singer would have had to show in order to follow his calling.

Furthermore, these men were not "ordinary" rabbis. On his father's side, they prided themselves on belonging to a long-standing Hasidic tradition. One of Singer's ancestors, Reb Moshe, was reputed to have been a disciple, in his day, of the renowned Baal Shem Tov, the father of Hasidism. This mystical, popular movement, founded in Poland in the second half of the eighteenth century, advocated a new conception of Judaism. Born in reaction to an impoverishment in traditional Jewish thought, it stressed an immediate and joyous communication with the divine and responded to a malaise within the poorest sectors of society, whose preoccupations had become increasingly estranged from the intellectual rigor of the rabbinate. Hasidism says that only the "worst ineptitude" can exempt a Hasid, a pious man, from embracing a rabbinical career. Isaac's first transgression was not to be his least.

His maternal ancestry was no less burdensome. Bathsheba Singer, Isaac's mother, born Zylberman, was also a rabbi's daughter. She came from Bilgoraj, a relatively large town on the Austrian frontier. We know less about the Zylbermans' genealogy than the Singers'. But the description of the grandfather in *In My Father's Court* paints a clear picture of the family landscape. Rabbi Zylberman was not one to waste his time on "pettiness or small talk; he gave his legal decisions or religious interpretations of the law, and said no more." The rest of the time, he asked to be left to study in peace. In Bilgoraj, writes Singer, "though there were always opposing parties trying to destroy each other in the affairs of ritual slaughterers, elders, flour for Passover, Community jobs," Grandfather Zylberman kept his distance. "Nothing but the Talmud and the eternal questions interested him."[8]

THE WHOLE WORLD SEEN AS UNCLEAN

Piety, austerity, severity—these were the golden rules of the Singer family, to which we might add saintliness, truth, and integrity. Time and time again, Singer described the ascetic climate of his youthful years. Whether he had indeed lived this way, or whether he merely remembered it this way, amounts to the same thing: he was born into what he called "a stronghold of Jewish puritanism." His childhood was spent in half-unfurnished homes where the pantry was bare. His parents weren't wealthy, but they also frowned upon the slightest sign of luxury. Carpets, paintings, statuettes—all were systematically banned as signs of wealth or idolatry. Faces and carved images be gone! Though children love illustrations—today we would say they help stimulate their imaginations—for the Singers it was never too soon to learn the obvious: you do not compromise with the Commandments.

"I remember that in the heder I had once bartered my Pentateuch for another boy's, because the frontispiece of his was decorated with pictures of Moses holding the Tablets and Aaron wearing the priestly robe and breastplate—as well as two angels. Mother saw it and frowned. She showed it to my father. Father declared that it was forbidden to have such pictures in a sacred book."[9]

The same discipline applied to the body, considered a "mere appendage to the soul." In fact, anything suggesting pleasure was banished. In his memoirs, Singer recounts how Purim—the holiday commemorating Queen Esther's role in saving the Jewish people— irritated his parents. On that day, the air smelled of cinnamon, saffron, and chocolate. Messengers brought the rabbi mead and sweet-and-sour fish. The guests arrived wearing masks and cardboard helmets covered with golden paper. For the young Isaac, this holiday was a magic moment. But his parents were dismayed by so much frivolity and extravagance. "Once a wealthy man sent us some English ale. Father looked at the bottle, which bore a colorful label, and sighed. The label showed a red-faced man with a blond mustache, wearing a hat with a feather. His intoxicated eyes were full of a pagan joy. Father said, in an undertone, 'How much thought and energy they expend on these worldly vanities.' "

This sort of intransigence marks a person for life, as does this conception of faith. It is either blindly adhered to or rejected outright. Any middle ground is impossible. Young Isaac must have understood this early on. During the Purim holiday, he was perplexed by this asceticism. Not only were all the cakes forbidden (there's no way of knowing if the laws of kashruth had been properly observed) but the masks were also thrown into the trash can. "The wearing of masks and the singing of songs smacked of the theater, and the theater was *tref*—unclean. In our home, the 'world' itself was *tref*."[10]

Anything that made one stray from the quest for God was unclean—theater, painting, literature. Becoming open to the secular world and its futile pleasures, failing to devote all one's energy to being a "good Jew," choosing the profession of writer—all were tantamount to deliberately choosing a wayward path, immoral and unclean. They were tantamount to betraying one's father and disavowing one's roots. This rebellion weighed heavily in the Singer legacy. In fact, the theme of betrayal recurs in his books like a leitmotif. Men and women spend their time mutually betraying one another. Children betray their parents; people betray their beliefs, their values, their gods. Worse, according to Singer, "men betray themselves," which, he says, bothers him "more than anything."[11]

Yet in interviews and in his writings, Singer never really dwelled on the guilt this transgression might have aroused in him. Was this because he hadn't felt any guilt? Or because he preferred to avoid the question? At seventy-four, in his conversations with Richard Burgin, then assistant professor of English at Drexel University and editor of the literary magazine *Boulevard*, he explained why he had rejected the rabbinate—because of his religious skepticism and because a rabbi's life was, in his eyes, "a miserable kind of life." He added, without committing himself further, that his father very much wanted him to follow in his footsteps, but that his "younger brother followed him instead."[12] This seems like a polite way of discouraging discussion. A bit later, when Burgin asked the question again, "Did your father feel a sense of betrayal because you and your older brother became writers?" Singer skillfully dodged the issue again. Rather than discuss his feelings, he chose to describe the specific requirements of Hasidism.

> Not only that we didn't want to be Rabbis, but that we left, from his point of view, our religion. From my father's perspective, I was an atheist, even though I believed in God. But he demanded more. I had to believe in every little dogma and bylaw the Rabbis created generation after generation. I had to believe that they were all given to Moses on Mount Sinai. However, I

could see that all these laws were man-made. For example, one law in the Bible became eighteen laws in the Mishnah and seventy in the Gemara or in the Book of Maimonides. This was their form of creativity. Just as the critics today will take a poem of Byron or Shelley and will write whole books about it, and they'll find in its verses things which the author never intended, so our Rabbis use the words of the Torah. They had to be creative, they had to do something with their minds, and after a while the Jewish people had to live according to this hair-splitting. They made life so difficult that a religious Jew had no time for anything else but religion. It became for the Hasidim and for many other Jews a twenty-four-hour-a-day job. I could see this when I was still very young. I also asked myself questions. If there is a God, why is it that those who pray and carry all these man-made burdens are often poor and sick and miserable and those who don't practice them are often happy? I saw at a very early age that this kind of religion is nothing but commentary upon commentary, sheer casuistry.[13]

Yet this did not prevent Singer from being a believer. All his life he insisted that he believed in God, but in his own way, without following any particular precepts. Had he been right to want to rid himself of this set of rules and constraints? Wasn't it an illusion to believe in an "in-between" area that is neither atheism nor strict observance? Singer asked himself these questions to his dying day. And like many of his heroes—some of whom ended their lives in Mea Shearim, the ultra-Orthodox neighborhood in Jerusalem—it is likely that these doubts accompanied him to the grave.

MISMATCHED PARENTS

But let us return to the precocious child who became convinced early on that man had perverted religion. Now he is a pale-faced little boy with red earlocks, growing up in "a stronghold of Jewish puritanism" under the protection of his two older siblings, Hinde Esther and Israel

Joshua, fourteen and eleven years older than he. In 1906, two years after Isaac's birth, a fourth and last child was born, Moishe, who later became a rabbi.

Their parents' marriage in Bilgoraj, several years before, had not gone unnoticed. Though it was almost summer, Singer's father, Pinchos Menahem, arrived in a fur coat. This detail is revelatory of his character. He was absentminded, inattentive, and naïve. He had been tied to his mother's apron strings and wore traditional long white hose and old-fashioned shoes. He wasn't at all interested in women and even less so in social customs. His mind was elsewhere. According to Singer, he could easily have taken his mother-in-law or sister-in-law as his wife that day. This is barely an exaggeration. Even for his own time, Pinchos Menahem had an unusual way of living in his own world. As a little boy, he had wanted to become a saint. As an adult, he devoted himself entirely to the Torah and couldn't stand the slightest disruption of his beloved study.

Pinchos Menahem's tragedy, however, was that he had neither his father's charisma nor his father-in-law's brilliance. Emotional and unworldly, he struggled to control his feelings. He was capable of bursting into tears, once predicting the end of the world when a woman swore a false oath on a sacred scroll. His detachment from reality may explain why he never succeeded in becoming an "official" rabbi. In the divided Poland of the day, he would have had to pass a Russian exam, but Pinchos didn't speak a word of Russian or Polish. He didn't even know how to write his address "in the letters of the Christians." He spoke only Yiddish and withdrew to his inner world, constantly insecure.

"Father always lived in the fear that he might, God forbid, be imprisoned. According to Russian law he was not even licensed to perform weddings or to grant divorces. True, by way of a certain 'fixer' he regularly sent small sums to the local precinct chief and captain. But who knows what the Russian police would suddenly decide to do?"[14]

Though Pinchos Menahem was a cultured man as far as tradition was concerned, Isaac never showed any admiration for him in his memoirs. On the contrary, he and his mother sometimes seemed ashamed of him. When he was called upon to arbitrate complex issues in the presence of wealthier rabbis, his wife worried in the kitchen, afraid that he wouldn't understand the complicated matters being discussed. Isaac, too, wondered about his father's capabilities and watched him with embarrassment. "My father, to be sure, presided at the head of the table, but he seemed to shrivel in the presence of these worldly divines and their smooth conversation . . . I resented these clever Rabbis, yet at the same time I envied their children."[15]

Bathsheba prompted no such feelings. At every opportunity in his autobiographical writings, Isaac expresses his love and deep admiration for his mother. This slim, well-dressed redhead with the smallest shoe size in town spoke in a learned way, and her words were always authoritative. While Pinchos Menahem was always in the background, a self-effacing, cowardly figure, Bathsheba was an unusually intelligent, capable woman with a strong personality. It is no coincidence that Singer invented the pseudonym Bashevis for himself in 1927 in her honor.

Bathsheba inherited wisdom and an interest in study from her father, Rabbi Zylberman. She learned Hebrew on her own, and read and reread, in the original, *Duty of the Heart*, *The Book of the Covenant*, and *The Straight Path*, books she kept at her bedside. She knew the Bible better than anyone. She was able to cite hundreds of rabbinical maxims and could even replace her husband if need be. She should have been a rabbi rather than a rebbetzin, the wife of a rabbi, a role that bored her and failed to satisfy her thirst for learning. According to Israel Joshua Singer, Pinchos and Bathsheba would have been better matched if she had been the husband and he the wife. "Even externally each seemed better suited for the other's role. Father was short and round, with a soft, fine, delicate face; warm blue eyes; full rosy cheeks; a small, chiseled nose; and plump, feminine hands. If not for the great reddish-brown beard and corkscrew-like earlocks, he would have resembled a woman. Mother, on the other hand, was tall and somewhat stooped, with large, piercing, cold-gray eyes, a sharp nose, and a jutting pointed chin like a man's."[16] Bathsheba rapidly sank into depression, or more precisely, a kind of caustic melancholy. Was it her confinement to the domestic sphere, or her lukewarm feelings for her husband that made her sad? With time, she became blunt and curt, as well as despondent, distant, and increasingly withdrawn.

Bathsheba clearly had not married Pinchos out of love. At sixteen, her father had given her the choice between two suitors: Pinchos Menahem, or the son of a rich family from Lublin. Bathsheba was said to have chosen the more erudite of the two. The marriage certificate, written in the Cyrillic alphabet, states that the ceremony was celebrated by her father, Rabbi Zylberman, in June 1889, year 5649 in the Jewish calendar. They formed such a bad pair that separation was discussed. Bathsheba's brothers urged her to leave this gentle dreamer, but by then the couple already had two children, Hinde Esther and Israel Joshua. In the end, they never divorced. Bathsheba and Menahem continued their marriage uninterrupted until the latter's death in 1929. The two were not so much together, but rather side by side, each cloistered in his or her own impermeable world. For Isaac, born into this atmosphere, the message was clear. He would have to create his own inner world very quickly, escape and protect himself from others, and rely primarily on himself.

FROM LEONCIN TO RADZYMIN

Singer was helped by a change in their lives. In 1907, after spending ten years in Leoncin, Pinchos Menahem was given the position of assistant to the rabbi of Radzymin. He was put in charge of the small yeshiva, or Talmudic school. Isaac was only three years old when the whole family set out for Radzymin. The two villages were a few miles apart, but the trip by wagon impressed the young Singer and worked its way into his imagination:

All the Jews in town came to bid us goodbye, and the women kissed Mother. Then we rode through fields, forests, and past windmills. It was a summer evening, and the sky seemed ablaze with blowing coals, fiery brooms, and beasts. There was a buzzing, a humming, and the croaking of frogs. The wagon halted, and I saw a train, first a large locomotive with three lamps like suns, then freight cars trailing behind in a slow, pre-occupied way. They seemed to come from nowhere and to go to beyond the end of the world, where the darkness loomed.

I began to cry. Mother said, "Why are you crying, silly? It's just a train." I know exactly what I saw at that time—a train with oil cars, but there was a sense of mystery about it then that still remains with me . . .[17]

Radzymin. Close to a century later, the ambience is less oppressive there than in Leoncin. In fact, if you go through the town today and ask the bookseller for a book on Radzymin, she spontaneously brings out a book by Singer. Then she tells you his address: "*Dom . . . Tak, tak . . . Stary Rynek, 7.*" Radzymin is a large town, about twelve miles northeast of Warsaw. Singer's house still stands on the main square, a sprawling building with a peeling façade and a wooden door, squeezed between a florist and greengrocer, steps away from the highway, the church, and the Solidarity delegation. The Friends of Radzymin Society even placed a plaque of the same gray as the façade on the building: "To Isaac Singer, an inhabitant of Radzymin, Nobel Laureate in Literature." The plaque is recent; it dates from 1991. Directly under it, in a makeshift stall, a jumble of cabbage, turnips, and carrots awaits the customer.

No one here knows Singer and no one seems to pay attention to his childhood home. "The plaque? What plaque?" exclaims a middle-aged Polish woman in impeccable French. "Singer, I don't know him," she says, glancing inquiringly at the group of women artists and intellectuals from Warsaw with whom she is spending a day in the country. One of them has read a few of his novels and short stories, but when asked whether she likes them, her astonishing reply is, "I like Jews. But, you know, Isaac Singer was particularly stingy."

Indifferent to this adult talk, a little boy and a grimy-nosed little girl are sitting on the sunken steps of the house. In the dark corridor, centuries of humidity assail visitors' noses. A worm-eaten wooden staircase looks as if it dates from the beginning of time. Beyond, a small garden shaded by an old walnut tree stretches along the length of the building. Sunflowers, a bicycle, turtle doves, a water pump in working order. Time seems to have stood still in Radzymin. One can easily recognize the town as it appears in the prewar photos collected in the *Livre du souvenir de la communauté juive de Radzymin*[18]—its unpaved streets, its two market squares, and the surrounding streets with wooden houses.

Isaac spent 1907 and 1908 in Radzymin, retaining photographic memories of those years. Here, we see him in an orchard, among currant and gooseberry bushes. There, he is at the heder learning the alphabet. There again, he is playing in the courtyard of his house or the rabbi's house, with Esther and Scheindele, his first female admirers. In those days, Radzymin had the same number of Jews as gentiles. The rabbi had the reputation of performing miracles, and people traveled from far and wide to see him. Yet this huge man with a yellowish beard wasn't at all generous with Pinchos Menahem, whom he clearly didn't like. He gave him a salary of a few rubles, doled out sporadically: the Singers lived in great poverty. But Isaac didn't seem to suffer from this. The young rebbetzin was fond of him. She gave him sweets and glass beads. Also, like many little boys his age, Isaac was curious about everything and already troubled by the larger questions.

"Standing there [in the orchard], I would gaze at the horizon. Was that the end of the world? What happened there and what was beyond it? What were day and night? Why did birds fly and worms crawl? I tormented my mother with questions. My father always answered, 'That's how the Lord made it.' "[19]

By this time, such answers no longer satisfied Isaac. An important aspect of those Radzymin years was precisely the intrusion of doubt. True, "the world is full of mysteries" and, as it says in the Kabbalah, "each thing contains the secret of secrets." But what if God wasn't the ultimate answer to all these questions? What if life wasn't a quest entirely focused on the pursuit of saintliness? Hinde Esther and Israel Joshua already seemed to wonder; they grew critical of the rabbi and religion. They imitated him shouting prayers and rolling his eyes as he distributed food to the Hasidim. Inevitably this influenced their younger brother.

So it was probably in Radzymin that, for Singer, the first crack began to appear in the "stronghold of Jewish puritanism." Soon there was another, more decisive one. In 1908, the Singers left Radzymin and moved to Warsaw. "Through the train windows," Isaac recalled, "I saw trees, buildings and people moving backwards."[20] He also remembered a sense of mystery that would never leave him—the idea that unintelligible things could exist, that there was a secret that he couldn't grasp. In leaving the country for the bustling city and turning from the observation of the external environment to that of human nature, the young Isaac plunged into a world that was no less obscure and enigmatic—the passions and dramas being played out in pre-1914 Jewish Warsaw on the stage of the immortal Krochmalna Street.

TWO

"The Gold Mine of Krochmalna Street"

HE COULDN'T HELP IT. He could be describing a New York sky, but inevitably Singer saw Polish clouds. He could be meditating in the courtyard of his building on the Upper West Side, yet there he was, transported to his native land; the only things missing, he said, were the peddler, the fortune-teller, and the hurdy-gurdy. By the time he died in Miami Beach in 1991, Isaac had spent fifty-six years—two thirds of his life—in the United States. But, almost always, his inspiration took him back to his youth in Warsaw. Yet it wasn't Warsaw in its entirety that interested him, or even the Jewish quarter; it was one lively street, and really only a tiny part of it, no more than a few houses of Krochmalna Street he would soon make famous.

Isaac spent nine years on that street, from 1908 to 1917, between the ages of four and thirteen. For writers, he would later say, "the first fifteen years of their life is never lost to them. It is like a well which is never exhausted."[1] In his case, everything started on Krochmalna Street and everything brought him back to it. The year he won the Nobel Prize, he said, "I keep going back to 10 Krochmalna Street in my writing. I remember every little corner and every person there. I say to myself that just as other people are digging gold which God has created billions of years ago, my literary gold mine is this street."[2]

Eventually the drill reaches the center of the Earth. Like Yoknapatawpha County for Faulkner, Singer keeps mining the same ground tirelessly, the same time period, among the same tiny group of humble people. His "nuggets" are all the more precious in that they tell us about a culture on the eve of its disappearance. Not just a "world of yesterday" in Stefan Zweig's sense, but a world that was leveled from the landscape of memory, impossible to reconstruct today. In his foreword to *In My Father's Court*, Singer tells us that even at an early age he always wanted to record his memories of Krochmalna Street. Did he realize how unique they were? Did he already sense that minutely detailed descriptions of that microcosm could give rise to stories that would free him from the closed world in which he was born and confer on him universal glory?

It hardly matters. Today the only thing that remains of the mythical Krochmalna Street is its name.[3] Almost nothing was spared by the World War II bombings. After the first ghetto uprising in 1943, the Nazis razed the houses. The last survivors were deported to Treblinka or Majdanek. The ground was leveled. A new neighborhood, cold and impersonal, sprang up on the site of the Jewish city.

"You search in vain for any traces of the past there," says the Polish historian Agata Tuszynska. She adds that years after the war, some people in Warsaw fought "to prevent the destruction of the remaining fragments of the ghetto wall between Sienna and Zlota Streets." But, she says, the Poles didn't "understand what the point was." After all, a monument to the heroes of the ghetto had already been erected with—thanks to the irony of history—blocks of granite ordered by Hitler for a monument to the glory of the Third Reich! Since 1988, there was also the Umschlagplatz monument, the "symbolic wall" on Stawki Street, where the Jews were rounded up before being deported: a structure in the shape of a freight car that bears the names of four hundred people, the only names remembered of the three hundred thousand who never returned. Why preserve any other memories? Weren't these sufficient? Agata Tuszynska suggests that the Poles didn't want any other reminders. During the forty-five years of communism after the Holocaust, "History has been erased . . . ; old landscapes have been nullified. Memory has been gagged."[4]

As of 2001, practically nothing remained in Warsaw of Singer's landscapes. Nothing but a long scar in the urban landscape: the Jewish cemetery of the former Gesia Street, a chaos of gravestones and vegetation magnificently immortalized by the photographer Hannah

Collins at the Tate Modern in London. The small Nozyk synagogue on Twarda Street is the only synagogue to have escaped destruction. There are a few modest, dilapidated brick buildings on Prozna Street, bought by the American foundation Jewish Renaissance, which is devoted to reviving Poland's Jewish past. Nearby, there is a surviving section of the ghetto wall at 59 Sienna Street, but there are no markers. You have to enter a courtyard, dimly lit by the blue light of television sets, to discover some twelve yards of brown brick and two commemorative plaques. *Mur ten byl granica getta*—"This wall was the boundary of the ghetto"—reads the inscription in Polish. Another, American plaque mounted in 1989 explains that two original bricks from this wall were taken to the United States Holocaust Memorial Museum in Washington, D.C., "to lend the power of authenticity to its permanent exhibits."

Sadder still is the fact that after the bulldozers came, the numbering on Krochmalna Street was changed. There is no No. 10 anymore. The numbers skip from 4 to 28—the taxi driver has no idea why. We find the explanation at the Warsaw Jewish Historical Institute. On a cadastral map drawn up by the Germans in 1943, the borders of the ghetto were delineated with a thin black line of tape like a death announcement: a city within the city fated to be wiped off the map. You can see on this map that in those days Krochmalna Street was three times longer than it is today. Knowing that the numbering in Warsaw starts at the Vistula and generally runs east to west, it should be possible to determine the location of No. 10. Opposite a picture framer and a stocking store? There are no official reminders of the Nobel Prize winner's existence. You can hear the sound of streetcars rolling by and bells chiming in the distance. On this warm summer evening, domestic noises drift from the buildings. But what of the old days? Soap and herring? The pale lighting of the inner courtyards? The song of the crickets? Almost nothing, really, and the taxi driver grows impatient.

"WITHOUT KNOWING TEN WORDS OF POLISH"

Reconstructing the pre–World War I setting requires great imagination. Try to visualize the *droshkys*—horse-drawn carriages—trundling over the cobblestones, weaving their way between the traps, the carts filled with cabbages and potatoes; to hear the crackling of the coachmen's whips or the clinking of the milk cans in the brisk early morning air; or to catch the sound of a Yiddish melody being played on an old gramophone between the noise of hammers and sewing machines. In Singer's day, Krochmalna Street was always in the grip of a kind of fever, teeming with life. Artisans, water carriers, furriers, tailors, fruit peddlers, fences, maids, witches . . . this was the colorful group of people you encountered who gave the street its motley flavor. In the connected courtyards of the buildings, children held top-spinning contests. Teenagers bought raffle tickets to win a *tchaste*—a chocolate-covered cracker; when their games turned rowdy a window would open and a woman would pour a pail of water on the adolescents. If you walked to the end of the street, you reached the ill-famed Krochmalna Square, the meeting place of thieves, pimps, and prostitutes. It was just a few steps away from the synagogues and the Hasidic study houses. Vice was never too far from virtue.

When they first arrived from Radzymin, the Singers settled at No. 10 Krochmalna Street; they moved to No. 12 six years later. The building was run-down. Its main characteristic, in Isaac's memory, was its dark, smelly staircase, which the other tenants used as a garbage dump. The lamps threw frightening shadows on the walls, so much so that this spot recurs like a nightmare in his autobiographical writings. "When I used this murky staircase, I was pursued by all the devils, evil spirits, demons, and imps of whom my parents spoke to prove to the older children that there was a God and a future life. Cats raced along beside me. From behind closed doors, one often heard a wailing for the dead."[5]

It is hard for us to imagine just how much of a city within the city the Jewish quarter was. Here, as opposed to Radzymin, contact with Christians was rare. The only goy in Singer's building was the janitor who came every Friday to earn his six groschen. There was also the washerwoman who carried huge bundles on her scrawny shoulders and who thought that little Isaac "looked like Jesus," a compliment that didn't particularly warm Bathsheba's heart. Aside from that, the quarter was like a country inside another country. This is confirmed by Szulim Rozenberg, one of the rare witnesses of the period. Born in Warsaw fourteen years after Singer on Armistice Day, November 11, 1918, Rozenberg had an intimate knowledge of Jewish Warsaw between the wars. He earned his living as a clerk in a wholesale shop. The elderly gentleman reminisced in a heavy Yiddish accent.

I used to live on Majzelsa Street, four or five hundred yards from Krochmalna Street. There were eighteen new houses there that had been built before my birth. Not a single one of them had a Polish tenant. Our whole life was conducted in Yiddish. We lived in a "Jewish country" with Yiddish newspapers, Yiddish schools, Yiddish theaters, Yiddish movie theaters . . . It was possible to live your entire life without knowing ten words of Polish. The same was true for the part of Krochmalna Street where Singer lived. At the end of the street, near Zelazna Brama Square, the square of the iron gate, you reached the Polish quarter and the Saxony Gardens and the bottom of Marszalkowska, the Champs-Élysées of Warsaw. At that point you were no longer in the Jewish city. But in Krochmalna Street, yes, of course you were. It was also the street where Janusz Korczak lived before he and his orphanage were deported in 1942.[6]

Rozenberg also described "the streetwalkers, opposite Singer's house, who were bad for the neighborhood," and the secular schools of the Bund—the Union of Jewish Workers from Lithuania, Poland, and Russia—where the neediest could send their children for modest sums of money. "Though even then," he added, "the director of the school made a point of bringing his shoes to the shoemaker every so often so he could keep on sending his son to the school." Though this was the Warsaw of the 1930s, Isaac would have recognized it immediately. The poor living conditions and the shabby housing, the daily deprivation, the collective poverty of the population were the very things he described in his works and that made his mother curse this "damned street" incessantly. The Singers rented an apartment overlooking the street for twenty-four rubles a month, without gas. They used kerosene lamps and shared vile toilets at the far end of the court-yard with the other residents in the building, both humans and rodents. Yet, in his recollections of those years prior to 1914, Singer seemed not to suffer from poverty. He even describes the holiday-like quality of Sabbath nights in wintertime. No. 10 Krochmalna Street was filled with the odor of burning wax and spices blessed by Pinchos Menahem. Sitting around the tile stove in their best clothes, the men sipped tea with lemon and discussed Hasidic matters.

FICTIONAL MATERIAL IN THE ROUGH

There is no doubt that for a child Isaac's age, No. 10 offered a permanent spectacle. Pinchos Menahem held a rabbinical court, or beth din, in the apartment. According to Singer's own definition, this ancient Jewish institution is a blend of a court of law, synagogue, house of study, and psychoanalyst's office. Pinchos Menahem arbitrated disputes, celebrated marriages, and granted divorces. It was also up to him to decide whether someone who had committed suicide could be given a decent burial, whether a young man could marry a repentant prostitute, or whether a chicken brought before him was really kosher. In short, he served as a kind of justice of the peace for countless daily dramas. Needless to say, he wasn't really cut out for this job. He resented being repeatedly torn away from his pious meditations and brought back to the crude vicissitudes of everyday life. For Pinchos Menahem it was infuriating: the beth din was such a burden. But one person in his entourage saw it differently: his son Isaac. Without saying a word, between two doors and a keyhole, the child absorbed every detail of what went on in his father's study. There, before his eyes, people came to plead their cases or pour out their hearts. They shouted, cursed, inveighed against one another. They went from laughter to tears; they kissed and made up. What a kaleidoscopic overview of life and passions! What a microcosm of humanity! Isaac couldn't believe his ears. All of this was so different from the disembodied austerity that had surrounded his family up until then. He wasn't about to forget these characters witnessed surreptitiously, these stolen stories. Indeed, he never forgot anything.

Before becoming his gold mine and the matrix of his work, Krochmalna Street was the young Isaac's laboratory. He was barely ten years old when he first started using life-size subjects to make subtle observations on the human soul. What did he discover? That "for most people there is only one small step between vulgarity and 'refinement,' between blows and kisses, between spitting at one's neighbor's face and showering him with kindness."[7] He tried to penetrate the mysteries, see through the ruses of the people he observed: "I remember trying to decide for myself which of them was honest and which of them was dishonest."[8] In other words, though he didn't know it, he was preparing to be a writer, like a musician practicing his scales. When he wasn't eavesdropping behind doors, he was on the balcony of the apartment; it was his favorite spectator's box, from which he fully absorbed the theatricality of the street scenes. From matrons in wigs to loud-mouthed and disheveled females, the women had the melodramatic airs of tragic actresses, the men impressive acting talent. "Indeed, there were couples on Krochmalna Street who would go out to the street when they wanted to fight and wait for a crowd to gather. What sense was there fighting in one's own apartment in front of the four walls?"[9] Fistfights, public arguments, stories of gangsters and prostitutes—what better fodder for the imagination? Did Pinchos Menahem say theater was *tref*, unclean? Unclean, perhaps, but exhilarating.

A YOUNG SCRIBE TAKES MENTAL NOTES

There was something of the "visionary filled with wonder" in the young Singer. Yet in this intense Krochmalna Street period, no full picture of him emerges. The self-portrait he draws is incomplete: a self-effaced mute witness who stores up the material that later becomes the source of his oeuvre. *In My Father's Court* covers the period from his earliest childhood to his adolescence, and in these three hundred–odd pages we really "see" him only in small glimpses and as a background figure. What is most important about these years is that he attended the school of life, thanks to his tireless observations of the beth din, which merged in his mind with life on the street. We are left with the profile of a little boy immersing himself in the strange and fascinating world of adults. Singer depicts himself as a painter standing in the background. It is a painting within a painting, a young scribe taking mental notes for the future. The scholar Éveline Thévenard-Cahn talks about this book as an "indirect autobiography" achieved through the "setting and the other protagonists," a sidelong glance that is more telling than a "long-drawn analysis of the Self." Behind the figures who left their marks on Singer in his childhood, she writes, "is the chorus of the shtetl population expressing itself, echoing and magnifying what the narrator-protagonist is thinking."[10]

What were the thoughts of the little boy in a satin gabardine and velvet hat who tried to penetrate the mysteries of the world from his Krochmalna Street balcony? No one really knows. What we do know is that these formative years were decisive; in this family interested solely in God and the Talmud, between a father absorbed in study and a relatively cold, detached mother, he broke through the silence of the sacred books and discovered the rich vibrancy of life through stories, legends, belief, and tales. From that time on, what he found most attractive, if not most authentic, lay on the side of the imagination. He must have felt as if the truth of life was entirely contained in the strangeness of fiction—a feeling that, as we will see, foreshadowed the subsequent part of his life rather well.

A MIXTURE OF THE REAL AND THE SUPERNATURAL

As might be expected, it was during his years on Krochmalna Street that Singer began to write—or rather, to "scribble." He covered pages and pages of white paper, pausing with reluctance only on the Sabbath. This was perhaps in part an imitation of what he saw. Everyone in the Singer household wrote except Bathsheba, who was a marvelous storyteller nonetheless. An unusual atmosphere, a mixture of the real and surreal hovering in the air they breathed, reigned in the Singer home, where the fantastic was constantly barging in on the staid world of the family circle: "In our home there was always talk about spirits of the dead that possess the bodies of the living, souls reincarnated as animals, houses inhabited by hobgoblins, cellars haunted by demons. My father spoke of these things, first of all because he was interested in them, and second because in a big city children so easily go astray. They go everywhere, see everything, read profane books. It is necessary to remind them from time to time that there are still mysterious forces at work in the world."[11]

For a little boy whose thirst for stories was already so strong, what greater happiness could there be than fables to make your earlocks stand on end? One such fable, titled "Why the Geese Shrieked," is a marvelous illustration of how the irrational could make a sudden appearance in the Singer household on any given day. While the family was gathered around Pinchos Menahem, the front door suddenly burst open. A woman came in, visibly distraught, carrying a basket with two dead geese. She explained that the geese had been slaughtered properly, but they kept screaming "sorrowfully." Singer's father turned pale and twisted his beard. Could this be the work of evil spirits? Isaac clung to his mother's skirts. As always, Bathsheba remained skeptical, an attitude that invariably exasperated her husband. Didn't she see it was a divine message? Pinchos Menahem began to moan, "Woe, woe, and still they blaspheme. They behold the truth with their own eyes, and continue to deny their Maker . . ." But after some reflection, Bathsheba laughed. Had the geese's windpipes been removed? The woman hesitated. His father reacted angrily again: What did windpipes have to do with the divine? Bathsheba stuck her finger down one of the geese's throats and pulled with all her might on the thin tube that led from the neck to the lungs. "I stood trembling, aghast at my mother's courage. Her hands had become bloodied. On her face could be seen the wrath of the rationalist whom someone has tried to frighten in broad daylight.

"Father's face turned white, calm, a little disappointed. He knew what had happened here: logic, cold logic, was again tearing down faith, mocking it, holding it up to ridicule and scorn." Afterward, in the kitchen, Isaac recorded the conclusions of each parent. Bathsheba said, "There is always an explanation. Dead geese don't shriek." Vexed, his father blurted out, " 'Your mother takes after your grandfather, the Rabbi of Bilgoray. He is a great scholar, but a cold-blooded rationalist. People warned me before our betrothal.' And then father threw up his hands, as if to say: It is too late now to call off the wedding."[12]

Once again, in these recollections, Singer the child remains in the background. He doesn't take sides. He never really chooses between the two currents running through the family, his father's mysticism and his mother's rationalism.[13] He straddles both sides, logic and magic. Yes, in this story he favors his mother. She has the last word. His father is a sorry, ridiculous figure. And yet things are not that simple. Singer often said he was convinced that higher powers existed. On Krochmalna Street, where, on the sly, he was already reading Kabbalah texts about demons, devils, and spirits, he lived, he said, "in dread fear of these invisible beings."[14] He acquired a profound respect for the mystery of things and the idea that nature is beyond our knowledge and includes the supernatural.

"I knew even as a child that the world which we see is not the whole world," he said when he received the Nobel Prize.

> Whether you call them demons or angels or some other name, I knew then, and I know today, that there are entities of whom we have no idea and they do exist. You can call them spirits, ghosts, or imps. Of course, I also use them as symbols in my writing. I can express with them many things which would be difficult for me to express if I only wrote about people. But this is not only a literary method, it is connected with a belief that the world is full of powers that we don't know. After all, let's not fool ourselves, a few hundred years ago we didn't know about microbes, we didn't know about electrons and those powers connected with radiation. So who says we have already come to the summit of knowledge?[15]

Particularly in his short stories, Isaac had a field day. Dancing corpses, bloodsucking monsters, tales of dybbuks, of incubi and succubi—it is impossible to give an exhaustive list of this very rich demonology.[16] Yet when he used the supernatural, Singer always situated his stories at the confluence of logic and the inexplicable, as if the story of the geese was permanently etched in his memory. He remained deliberately ambiguous, he said, not unlike Edgar Allan Poe in his short stories. It was his way of being elsewhere, in several places at once, on both his father's side and his mother's simultaneously.

The young Isaac of Krochmalna Street was already a mystical realist. He had all the dualities, in embryonic form, of the mature writer. He admired the supernatural but respected logic. He believed in the divine but distrusted orthodoxy. He was basically a believer but sought proof of God's existence. Even more than in Radzymin, he wondered about all sorts of things. He was tormented and eager to understand. Krochmalna Street was not only an inexhaustible spectacle but also an eternal source of questions. Did the proximity of synagogues and whorehouses illustrate the necessary cohabitation of good and evil? Why did the Russians make pogroms against the Jews? Why weren't all the Hasidim honest people? Would he recognize the Messiah when he rode in on his donkey one day, as he was told? There were also questions of a more scientific nature: How had nature become what it is? What went on deep inside the Earth? Not to mention the mystery of mysteries: What went on inside his own head? Why was he, a little blue-eyed redhead, assailed by these nagging questions?

The answers eluded him. Sometimes he saw his mother return from the market with lambs' brains. "Could my brains be cooked and eaten, too?" he wondered. "Yes, of course, but so long as they weren't cooked, they kept on thinking and wanting to know the truth."[17]

A MENTOR AND A MASTER

In his agonizing quest for truth, Isaac soon found an influential ally: his brother, Israel Joshua. Joshua was twenty when Isaac was nine. Until Joshua's death in 1944, he remained the admired older brother and mentor, but Isaac envied him as well. Joshua was the kind of model one is drawn to but must also distance oneself from. For the time being, Isaac listened to Joshua's discussions with Bathsheba. He espoused Cartesianism and rationalism even more than she did.

Joshua believed in neither God nor the devil. He read "heretical" books, believed the universe was millions and millions of years old, that man descended not from Adam but from the ape, that God didn't create the world in six days but that the Earth had originally been part of the sun and tore away. He spent his time in libraries, museums, and theaters, and with women. He painted portraits and wrote stories he called literature. To a nine-year-old boy, such a free spirit was irresistible. Isaac, ransacking his father's bookshelves for answers to his enigmas, discovered the theories of Copernicus and Newton, as well as stories about savage tribes. New horizons opened up to him. Joshua encouraged him to go much further in exploring these new paths. "My urge to know what the unbelievers or the scientists had to say grew ever stronger. Who knows—perhaps the truth lies with them? A Jewish publisher in Warsaw had begun to issue a series of popular books on science, and I asked my brother to bring them to me. My brother and I now shared a secret."[18]

Thanks to Joshua, Isaac discovered physics and astronomy. Even more important, he was initiated into the world of literature. What had he read up to then? Holy books, Hebrew texts, and especially the Kabbalah behind his father's back, because it was forbidden at his age. He adored the Kabbalah, because it reminded him that "everything is God and God is everything . . . the stone in the street, the mouse in its hole, the fly on the wall . . ."[19] No one knows at exactly what age he discovered secular writing. *In My Father's Court* alludes to stories about emperors, caves, and thieves. But the first secular title he specifically mentions is a collection of Sherlock Holmes stories in Yiddish translation. Years later, Singer said he never wanted to reread these stories for fear of being disappointed. How had Conan Doyle entered the household? Thanks to Joshua? Be that as it may, a few years later, his older brother brought him a copy of *Crime and Punishment*. Isaac was twelve years old; the novel made an indelible impression on him. Though he says he understood "very little of it," only that the hero had committed a murder, he found some of it "wonderful."[20] A loyal admirer, Singer continued to love Dostoyevsky, Tolstoy, Gogol, and Chekhov (his favorite short-story writer) for the rest of his life. At twelve he was giddy at the discovery of a new way of explaining the world—literature. Encouraged by the librarian on Nowolipki Street, his appetite for stories grew. Once again, pleasure vied with fear. He was afraid of transgressing, of "becoming a heretic." He also had the strange feeling of being in several places at once and of being different from other children his age.

> I existed on several levels. I was a heder boy, yet I probed the eternal questions. I asked a question about the Gemara and tried to explain the mysteries of Zeno. I studied the cabala and I went down to play tag and hide-and-seek with the boys in the courtyard . . . I was aware of being quite different from all the other boys, and I was deeply ashamed of this fact. Simultaneously I read Dostoevski in Yiddish translation and penny dreadfuls that I bought on Twarda Street for a kopeck. I suffered deep crises, was subject to hallucinations. My dreams were filled with demons, ghosts, devils, corpses. Sometimes before falling asleep I saw shapes. They danced around my bed, hovered in the air. In my fantasies or daydreams I brought the Messiah or was myself the Messiah.[21]

THE FIRST WORLD WAR AND THE SILENCE OF GOD

Between 1908 and 1916, the child who was curious about everything and fascinated by discovering the world gradually turned into a tormented adolescent subject to abrupt mood changes. In this strange climate, a blend of mysticism and doubt, piety and rationalism, reality and the supernatural, another decisive rupture occurred—the First World War. After those radiant, albeit penniless, years on Krochmalna Street, the world was suddenly turned upside down. Memories of holiday evenings and lively Sabbaths soon gave way to hunger, cold, and hardship.

Isaac was about to celebrate his tenth birthday when, on June 28, 1914, Archduke Francis Ferdinand, the heir to the Austro-Hungarian throne, was assassinated in Bosnia. Several weeks later, at the end of July, Austria declared war on Serbia. Europe was set ablaze; the First

World War broke out. Poland was reborn and became independent four years later, on the ruins of the powers that had torn it apart. But until the end of 1917, Poland's position was untenable. Each power thought it could break its promises and grab the other's share; each tried to find Polish groups favorable to its "protection." In the meantime, thousands of Poles killed one another fighting on opposing sides, Russian and Austro-Hungarian. By the end of the war, Poland's three partitions had lost at least four hundred thousand soldiers.

During the first year, from July 1914 until the German occupation of Warsaw in August 1915, the war remained relatively abstract. For a ten-year-old boy, it even had its exciting aspects. Isaac was haunted by the ghost of Gavrilo Princip, the nineteen-year-old high school student who, at such a young age, had killed the archduke and his wife. There was talk of cannons that could take down thousands of men at once, of the airplane, an engine lighter than air, successfully flown by the Wright Brothers ten years earlier in the United States, which people predicted would play an important role in the conflict. War also offered the opportunity of forging more breaches in the "stronghold of Jewish puritanism." It became possible, for example, to obtain world news. Until 1914, Isaac had to read the Yiddish newspapers, borrowing them secretly from the tinsmith Moshe Blecher. For Pinchos Menahem, as one would suspect, "the newspapers were full of blasphemy and heresy. He said that to start the day by reading the paper was like eating poison for breakfast."[22] But suddenly, now that the armies were fighting close to nearby villages, Pinchos Menahem started reading the news. The Yiddish newspapers lacked the necessary technical terms, relying on Russian or German words for "strategy" or "tactic." The family followed the progression of the German armies with growing alarm.

"Father gripped his red beard while his blue eyes gazed out the window and up to heaven. They fought and shed blood over some poverty-stricken village, some muddy stream. They burned the wooden shacks and the meager possessions of the paupers who often had to flee into the cold nights with their children. I heard Father mumble: 'Woe, woe is us, God in heaven!' "[23]

Soon every trace of excitement vanished. On July 5, 1915, the German Ninth Army entered Warsaw. Two weeks later, it captured the Russian stronghold on the Vistula, near Brest-Litovsk. In the course of a few months, the balance of forces on the Eastern front changed completely. When the Russians retreated, Poland was partitioned into two occupation zones—the Austrian zone, near Lublin, and the German zone, which included Warsaw. The situation worsened considerably. The loss of the Russian market, compounded by the confiscation of the means of production, struck a heavy blow to the Polish economy. The Jews, primarily artisans and owners of small businesses, were the first to suffer. Former shopkeepers opened bars or became street vendors. Large numbers of people fled the German invasion to seek asylum in Russia: Christian and Jewish Poles, along with Ruthenians, Latvians, Lithuanians—in the words of a newspaper at the time, "an entire Babel set out on the road." The situation soon deteriorated further. The Germans instituted the system of preference for the *Vaterland*, the country of origin, which made their own interests prevail over all others and brought even greater ruin to Poland. The rise in prices led to strikes and famines. Typhus broke out and mortality rates skyrocketed. The winter of 1916 was particularly dreadful, as Isaac recalled it. It was bitter cold. The pipes froze. The Singers were dying of hunger and thirst. Several months before, Moishe had become ill with typhus. He recovered after being taken to the communal hospital, where Bathsheba cried her heart out. In his quest for truth, Isaac witnessed an explosion of barbarity and violence beyond his grasp.

> Between 1915 and 1917, hundreds of people died on Krochmalna Street. Now a funeral procession passed our windows and now the ambulance taking the sick to the hospital. I saw women shake their fists at the sky and in their rage call God a murderer and a villain. I saw Hasidim at the Radzymin study house and in the other study houses grow swollen from malnutrition. At home we ate frozen potatoes that had a sweetish, nauseating taste. The Germans kept scoring victories, but those who foretold that the war wouldn't last longer than six weeks had to admit their error. Millions of people had already perished, but Malthus' God still hadn't had enough.[24]

Thus the war raised more questions in Isaac's mind. In his memoirs there is very little about the major events of 1916, such as the death of Francis Joseph, emperor of Austria, or Rasputin's assassination. Most striking is his quest for understanding. At twelve he threw himself so wholeheartedly into reading that he forgot the torments of hunger. He was eager to discover, he said, "why men and animals had to suffer" and the mystery of "the creation of the world."[25] He devoured philosophy books in Yiddish, which he borrowed on Nowolipki Street, but they left him dissatisfied. He noted that Locke, Hume, and Kant admitted they didn't know everything. He even suspected them of masking "their ignorance behind Latin and Greek phrases."[26] In his "spiritual autobiography," we "see" him clearly, this precocious child, thirsting for knowledge, enraged at being unable to find answers to the questions haunting him. Feelings of helpless confusion all around him were no less great. As always in the Singer family, everything came back to God. How could He permit such suffering? Since "the Lord of the Universe is a merciful and compassionate God,"[27] how could He allow famines, epidemics, pogroms? In her despair, Bathsheba spent most of her time in bed. Pinchos Menahem said nothing. Joshua quarreled with both of them.

To add to the chaos, the Russian Revolution broke out. In March 1917, Nicholas II ordered the army to crush the workers' strike that blocked Petrograd. The soldiers refused to obey and fraternized with the insurgents. Several days later, the czar abdicated. The press announced the return to Russia of Oulianov, "a paunchy little man with ferret eyes," better known as Lenin, who advocated the socialization of the country. All of Europe followed the events of these historic days. On May 1, the people of Petrograd took to the streets to celebrate the great revolutionary holiday. There was immense enthusiasm. "The speeches were in tune with the music," reported the correspondent of *L'Illustration*, trying to convey the prevailing state of mind. "It is the apotheosis of peace, the proletariat, and international brotherhood. The worldwide tragedy with its bloody convulsions, the nations gasping under the Prussian boot . . . memories of the war, its menace and ghosts, everything is forgotten. The only enemy now is the bourgeois, the Russian capitalist, and the Entente enemy, which is seen as thirsting for annexations and compensations."[28]

Predictably, this fervor spread to Poland. In the small industrial towns, where many workers were Jewish, the social agitation gained a new impetus and became more violent, echoing the Russian Revolution. Among Warsaw's poor as well, the downfall of czarism was synonymous with hope. Some people in Singer's entourage even went so far as to see it as an "act of Providence" or—why not?—as an "omen presaging the coming of the Messiah." But Singer, as clearheaded as ever, noted that the dead continued to "rot" before his eyes.[29] By the summer of 1917, the situation had become intolerable. Bathsheba decided to take her two younger sons, Isaac and Moishe, to her parents in Bilgoraj. Meanwhile, Singer's father returned to Radzymin, to the rabbi who had been his former employer. Joshua didn't want to leave Warsaw; he had been dating Genia, the young woman who would soon become his wife. Hinde Esther, married, had already left home. The Singer family fell apart. Isaac was thirteen. He left behind his beloved Krochmalna Street, where he had seen the faces of good and evil, as inseparable as two sides of a coin. He left Warsaw, to return six years later after a crucial journey of inner exploration.

THREE

A *"Private War Against the Almighty"*

In the summer of 1917, the journey to Bilgoraj was a return to life. Hunger, illness, and deprivation vanished. For the adolescent Isaac, the train was "a paradise on wheels,"[1] transporting him, his brother, and his mother away from the sufferings of war to a new promised land. Joshua had taken them to the Warsaw station by *droshky*. The steam engine, its black wheels dripping with oil, took two days and two nights to reach Bilgoraj in Lublin province.

Isaac had not left Warsaw for nine years; the briefest excursion outside the Jewish quarter had been an adventure for him. At thirteen, he yearned to be elsewhere. He "was overflowing with modern rebelliousness and a mad desire for upheaval, extraordinary news, weird changes . . ." In *More Stories from My Father's Court* he admits to having briefly imagined his father's beard cut off by "a pair of scissors or a razor"![2] How revealing of his ambivalent feelings: deeply attached to his cultural heritage, Isaac nonetheless longed to start fresh. He was already the "eternal outsider," forever at odds with his background.[3]

However, at this point in time he was ecstatic. The departure intoxicated him. Relief at escaping the war was coupled with a strange sense of power. He compared himself to "a king or a great wizard" riding through the world, "no longer fearing every soldier, policeman, Gentile boy, or bum."[4] He had colorful, romantic images of Bilgoraj in his head: officers dancing with Russian women; Cossacks riding "whip in hand through the streets, wearing a single earring and round caps."[5] His sightings from the train substantiated and complemented all the things his mother had told him. The glittering crosses of Warsaw's Russian Orthodox church, the fields, pastures, and sap-filled trees, a scarecrow standing "like an idol" "in the midst of the field." This journey remained even more vividly etched in his memory than the trip from Radzymin to Warsaw; he remembered the landscape gliding before his eyes "as if the earth were a huge carousel."[6] The magnificent promise of life beckoned.

Yet signs of war were ubiquitous. At Ivangorod, in Austrian territory, the station teemed with soldiers. In a detail typical of a childhood memory, Isaac noted that they "were not as tall, erect, or stiff-backed as the Germans." Indeed, Austro-Hungary was firing its final shots. A year later, what Robert Musil called *Kakanien*, the *kaiserliche-königliche Monarchie*, would come to an end. Isaac remembered the soldiers' puttees and the face of one of them, a Yiddish-speaking Galician Jew who allowed Moishe to hold his sword and try on his cap. Destroyed villages, charred forests—evidence of the czar's army's retreat was everywhere. In Rejowiec, there was a Russian prisoner-of-war camp where he saw "unarmed Russians with unkempt hair and shabby uniforms digging under Austrian guard."[7] But none of this affected Isaac's elation, or his romantic perspective. His thoughts, he said, "sped on with wheels, stimulated by every tree, shrub, and cloud." The smell of pine needles intoxicated him. He "wished that like some hero in a storybook" he might "leap from the moving train" and lose himself amid "green things."[8] In these minute details we see the writer's mind already at work. The world constantly appealed to his imagination. All his senses were on the alert; he saw himself as the protagonist in a novel. Transforming his destiny, like all great writers, he was already reinventing his life and staging it, refashioning it into the material for a novel with himself as hero.

AN INWARD JOURNEY

Warsaw, Ivangorod, Rejowiec, Zwierzyniec, and finally . . . Bilgoraj. The village looked like the ones in early Chagall paintings: surrounded with pinewoods "like a blue sash," dotted with yellow and green fields, log houses painted white and clustered around the synagogue. Whom would they find there? In Warsaw, Bathsheba had dreamt that her father had died. On the train, before arriving, she met people from Bilgoraj who recognized her as "the rabbi's Bathsheba." They confirmed her premonition. Not only had her father died of cholera in Lublin, where he had moved to escape from the Russians, but her mother, Hannah, had died, too. One of her sisters-in-law, Sarah, her brother Joseph's wife, had also died during the epidemic, as had one of their daughters. Singer notes how upset his mother was by this news. "I too tried to cry, feeling it appropriate," he writes, seeing himself as a little actor playing a part, "but the tears would not come. I cheated, wetting my eyes with saliva . . ."[9]

It is true that he had barely known the grandparents he had lost. And he had never seen the uncles, aunts, and cousins he was about to meet in Bilgoraj. These included Joseph, his mother's brother, who had inherited the rabbi's position, and Joseph's third wife, Yentl, as well as his mother's younger brother, Itche, his wife, Rochele, and six cousins—Avromele, Brocha, Taube, Esther, Moshele, and Samson, the only one who would survive the Holocaust.

On the surface, the years in Bilgoraj—where Isaac stayed until 1921 and later returned for short periods in 1922 and 1923—seem to symbolize a return to family and tradition. But as Éveline Thévenard-Cahn points out, those years actually conceal another journey. Away from the closed, theatrical world of the rabbinical court, Singer began to explore the outside world and its different modes of thought, from the Jewish to the gentile world; the Bilgoraj period further widened the cracks in the "stronghold of Jewish puritanism." Singer continued what he had started to do on Krochmalna Street, opening himself up to new ideas, but this time with passion, as befitted a boy about to become a young man. After the discovery of his community, Bilgoraj became the occasion for soul-searching: an inward journey that led him to formulate an unusual relationship with God and soon gave rise to a double initiation: literary and emotional.

The context certainly lent itself to soul-searching. In 1917, Bilgoraj was virtually cut off from the world. The villagers guarded the traditions of earlier times. There were no Yiddish newspapers in the town.

Rabbi Zylberman had done his job well. He "had insulated Bilgoraj against evil temptation." Every Jew prayed three times daily, and all the married women cut off their hair.[10] Though "the Enlightenment" had come to Lithuania a hundred years earlier, Bilgoraj still practiced centuries-old Judaism. On Thursday, market day, peasants in sheepskins came to sell potatoes and lumber. "Enlightened" Jews were few—no one seemed to have heard, for instance, of the great Yiddish writer Isaac Leib Peretz, a native of the region, whose death in Warsaw two years earlier had set off a virtual national mourning period. News of the world trickled in, in filtered form. In the fall, Bilgoraj learned that the Reds had entered Petrograd and stormed the Winter Palace. Trotsky had announced the abolition of landownership. But for Isaac, all of this was very remote. "A new Russian revolution was rumored and we heard that the rich were sweeping floors and lighting stoves for the poor. But for a long time I did not see a newspaper. No matter what happened in other parts of the world, Bilgoray remained unaltered beneath mud and fog."[11]

Singer never became interested in socialism or Marxism, though it was in Bilgoraj that he read *Das Kapital* in Yiddish. Materialism— particularly historical materialism—did not attract him, he said. Just as he had thrown off the shackles of religion as a child and rebelled against his strict family Orthodoxy, so, too, as an adolescent he distrusted all forms of utopia. He hated ideologies and systems, and spoke with disdain of all of those -isms (Marxism, socialism, and Zionism) which he found false and ridiculous. Yet they were thriving in Poland at the time. In that pivotal period of the 1920s, two years after the proclamation of independence, the Jews were the first to be drawn to these movements. The great majority, particularly the most destitute, were Communists or Zionists—often both. Even Israel Joshua had been won over. In 1918 he was in Ukraine working for a Yiddish newspaper, *Di Naye Tayt* (The New Times). He and Genia Kupferstok, who had become his wife, participated in the "literary research of the 'Kiev Group.'" By 1919 he had moved to Moscow and was as enthusiastic a supporter of Bolshevism as some of the protagonists of his future novels.

With time, the winds of change reached Bilgoraj, but Isaac himself remained impervious to them. He preferred devoting himself to loftier subjects, endlessly pondering the eternal questions, dissecting the world and its mysteries, and reading day in and day out. A watchmaker in Bilgoraj called Todros, not unlike Jekuthiel in *The Family Moskat*, practiced humanism and atheism. Singer had endless discussions with this enlightened man about good and evil, spirits, the existence of God, time and space, and the origin of nature. Thanks to Todros, who received scientific periodicals from Warsaw, Singer discovered Albert Einstein and Max Planck. They discussed atoms, electrons, the infinity of the universe, and cosmology. While the rationalist Todros did not believe in the existence of God, Singer, deeply religious, rose up against a God who tolerated man's savagery without flinching. How could a benevolent God desire this? With the same slightly naïve disapproval he expressed even in old age, the young Isaac believed that if "God wants or feels compelled to torture His creatures, that is His affair," but it was out of the question for him to personally support killings and slaughter.[12]

A PHILOSOPHY OF PROTEST

Singer's "ethic of protest," a philosophy that would be his to the end, was born in Bilgoraj. Coupled with a way of living that he said explained his later decision to become a vegetarian, the point was to show God that he disapproved of the way He ran the world, disapproved of His silence and absence of compassion. In *A Little Boy in Search of God*, Singer insists that because God is evil, man should behave in a moral way. What purpose does this serve? None, except "to spite God." For "if God kills and man kills, too, it means," says Singer, "that we approve of the killing, and we can no longer blame God for the evils of the world."[13]

Throughout his life, Singer referred to what he called his "private war against the Almighty."[14] With time, he developed the idea, systematized it, and went so far as to make it a basic feature of his personality. At eighty-one, in a conversational exchange with Anthony Burgess, he stressed yet again the compassion he said he felt since childhood for all suffering creatures. He asserted that compassion and rebellion were his two main character traits. He even told Burgess that, on occasion, God contained the devil. Hence he waged war against Him tirelessly.[15]

The most striking thing about Singer's resentment of God is its permanence. In 1978, in his conversations with Richard Burgin, Singer repeated the thoughts he had expressed already in the 1920s. The colorful and naïve wording, the disillusioned humor, did not change. But with hindsight, and especially after the genocide of the Second World War, Singer went further:

> I often say to myself that God *wants* us to protest. He has had enough of those who praise Him all the time and bless Him for all His cruelties to man and animals.
>
> I have written a little book which I call *Rebellion and Prayer* or *The True Protester*. It is still in Yiddish, untranslated. It was written at the time of the Holocaust. It is a bitter little book and I doubt that I will ever publish it. Yes I am a troubled person, but I am also joyful when I forget (for a while) the mess in which we are stuck. I may be false and contradictory in many ways, but I am a true protester. If I could, I would picket the Almighty with a sign: "Unfair to Life."[16]

FROM SPINOZA TO KNUT HAMSUN

Unfair to life? Yet there were many good things about Singer's stay in Bilgoraj. First, his immersion in literature. In this village cut off from the world, what else could one do but read? Singer did so with delight. Under the apple tree in the garden, or in his grandfather's house, he read everything he could get his hands on. He combed through old physics textbooks, discovered Archimedes and Pascal in German, studied a Russian dictionary, started to read in Polish and Hebrew. At sixteen, he wrote his first poem—in Hebrew. He later said, "Its poetic value was nil, but the Hebrew was good."[17]

It was also in Bilgoraj that he discovered the Yiddish writers

Mendele Mocher Seforim, Sholem Aleichem, Isaac Leib Peretz, and Sholem Asch, along with Hillel Zeitlin, whose book *The Problem of Good and Evil* completely enthralled him. He became infatuated with the poetry of Hayim Nahman Bialik and Saul Tchernikhovsky. And then there was everything else. At the time, America sent Poland sacks of flour and Yiddish translations of European writers. These books delighted him. After *Crime and Punishment*, he immersed himself in Russian literature—Turgenev, Tolstoy, and Chekhov—refining his critical faculties in the process. "Now, under the apple tree in the garden, Notte Shverdsharf would bring me a book one day and I would finish it the next. Often, sitting on an overturned bookcase in the attic, I would read among old pots, broken barrels, and stacks of pages torn from the sacred books. Omnivorously, I read stories, novels, plays, essays, original works in Yiddish, and translations. As I read, I decided which was good, which mediocre, and where truth and falsity lay."[18]

It was also at this time that he made one of his most significant discoveries: Spinoza. The Dutch philosopher was not entirely unfamiliar to him. Several years earlier he had discovered his theories in a dictionary of philosophers borrowed from the Nowolipki Street Library in Warsaw. He had detected then a similarity between Spinoza and the Kabbalah, but now the *Ethics*—in German—had a profound effect on him. "As I read this book, I felt intoxicated, inspired as I never had been before. It seemed to me that the truths I had been seeking since childhood had at last become apparent. Everything was God—Warsaw, Bilgoray, the spider in the attic, the water in the well, the clouds in the sky, and the book on my knees. Everything was divine, everything was thought and extension . . . I too was a modus, which explained my indecision, my restlessness, my passionate nature, my doubts and fears."[19]

We should try to imagine this young man of sixteen, with a pale complexion, blue eyes, and reddish earlocks. He wore a long gabardine coat; his head was filled with novels and poetry; he was excited by Spinoza, exhilarated by literature. Given this state of mind, it is hardly surprising that he had no desire to go live with his father. It was 1920. Pinchos Menahem had left Radzymin to become the rabbi of Dzikow, not far from Bilgoraj. Bathsheba and Moishe were going to join him, but Isaac wasn't at all attracted to shtetl life. After much discussion, his parents agreed to let him return to Warsaw on the condition that he begin rabbinical studies. So, in 1921, he entered the Tachkemoni Seminary, a kind of undergraduate school. He attended for only a year, later calling it one of the worst periods of his life. He had no permanent home, no money, and above all, he was dreadfully bored. Unable to concentrate on the religious subject matter, he read secular literature even more voraciously. With *Hunger*, he discovered Knut Hamsun, whom he repeatedly said had an influence on his future as a writer. This was the only outstanding event of that period. Singer never graduated from the seminary. In 1922 he left Tachkemoni and returned to Bilgoraj.

"THE TURMOIL THAT WRITERS CALL 'LOVE'"

This time Isaac was alone in Bilgoraj. He survived by teaching Hebrew, never expecting to have his first experiences of love thanks to these lessons. There were many young girls among his students, including Todros's daughter. They were pretty, well dressed, gathering around him to ask questions after class. Though Isaac was shy and introverted, only a zombie could have been immune to their charms.

This was not Isaac's first experience of "the turmoil that writers call 'love.' "[20] He had first experienced it in Warsaw, several years before, on a visit to Joshua's art studio. At the time, Joshua wanted to paint, and through him Isaac had discovered a true "Garden of Eden." Girls posed nude in front of him "with no more shame than they would have about undressing in their own bedrooms." Singer remembers being amazed at the sight of these bodies: "I was astonished at the sight of naked breasts on the figures of young and pretty girls, for I had assumed that breasts were solely the property of slovenly women who nursed babies in public."[21]

In Bilgoraj, however, his discoveries were not anatomical but emotional. Isaac experienced the first feelings of love. Sometimes his head spun so much that he thought he "was going crazy, or was possessed by a dibbuk." In sum, he had become, as he himself said, "aware of the female sex."[22] Knowing the importance of women in his life and work, that year was a crucial turning point—and it was all thanks to Hebrew! Meanwhile, his lessons caused a scandal, for he was teaching the sacred language with a completely secular goal . . . and to girls, no less! But this was far from displeasing to him. The interplay between the pure and impure involved just the kind of paradoxical delights he adored: "In my stories," he later noted, "it is just one step from the study house to sexuality and back again. Both phases of human existence have continued to interest me."[23]

A RETURN TO WARSAW

In 1922, Isaac fell ill and had no choice but to join his family in Dzikow. His brother Moishe had become extremely pious and was planning to become a rabbi. Through him, Isaac discovered the "wondrous tales" of the great Jewish mystic Rabbi Nachman of Breslov.[24] But apart from that he felt bored. He didn't quite know what to do with his life. At eighteen, he had fled the rabbinical seminary with no plans for the future. He had written only a few poems, which he considered mediocre. What would become of him?

Once again his brother Joshua came to his aid. Two years earlier Joshua had returned from Moscow with his wife, Genia, and their two-year-old son, Yasha. His stay had ended up making him critical of communism. Apparently his Russian publishers had printed his short stories without paying him royalties. But what alarmed him most was the Bolshevik terror. He preferred to return to Poland, where he was well connected in literary circles. He was even a member of a new avant-garde. With the Moscow writer Peretz Markish and the Viennese writer Melech Ravitch, he had founded a journal called *Khaliastra* (The Gang), which would soon draw other writers and poets, including Joseph Opatoshu and Oser Warszawki, as well as painters such as Itzik Brauner, Marc Chagall, and Victor Weintraub, whose constructivist and expressionist drawings and engravings were the pride of the new Yiddish modernity, finding an audience in

Berlin, Moscow, Kiev, New York, and Paris.[25] Freed from the fashionable Soviet aesthetic, Israel Joshua now wrote personal and varied works of great literary quality. In 1923, his play *Erd-vey* (Earth Cry) was produced at the Yiddish Art Theater in New York, garnering him fame outside Poland. In short, his literary career was well on its way when, in 1923, after the birth of his second son, Joseph, he became coeditor of the Warsaw journal *Literarische Bletter* (Literary Pages).

This is what changed Isaac's fate. Forever attentive, Joshua continued to advise and encourage his younger brother. As soon as Joshua started work at the *Literarische Bletter*, he wrote and offered Isaac a position as proofreader. Isaac welcomed the opportunity to put an end to his nine months' stay in Dzikow. In 1923, he boarded the train for Warsaw, where he would remain until 1935. He had left six years earlier, as an adolescent, the year of his bar mitzvah. Now he was a young man, still exploring the mysteries of the world and himself, about to begin his first job. In the interval, Bilgoraj, the "promised land" of his dreams, had led him to the paths of God, love, and literature. The three main focal points of his work were in place, three focal points that were in fact one—religion, love, and even sexuality, all "aspects of the same thing."[26] At nineteen, the young Isaac was ready to throw himself heart and soul into the service of what he called his two "idols," the two causes he would thereafter serve unfailingly: women and literature.[27]

FOUR

"The Servant of Two Idols"

WHAT WAS HE LIKE, this nineteen-year-old youth who made his way into the Warsaw "Literary Pages" by the back door in 1923? He was as thin as a scarecrow, had a malicious twinkle in his blue eyes, and was a marvelous imitator of his editor in chief's mannerisms. He kept his distance and observed everything. He had a critical mind, but he also lacked self-confidence. He had the reserve of the proud and the boldness of the timid. He was full of contradictions. One of the rare survivors from that period, Samuel Shneiderman, a former journalist with the *Literarische Bletter*, was struck by the paradoxes that already defined Singer: his sense of humor was rooted in a solid serious-mindedness; his impressive erudition didn't prevent him from staying somehow "outside things"; his mysticism went hand in hand with a "healthy suspicion" of religion. Shneiderman describes him as a solitary and secretive young man: "I never visited him at home—there was no home to visit. Just a succession of rooms where he never invited anyone. We were never, in fact, close friends. Isaac has had very few close friends. I remember he even looked like a hermit, but a special kind of hermit. A hermit with a lust for living, a passion for women, a strong desire to travel, to know the world."[1]

Singer's last years in Poland, 1923 to 1935, were marked by this duality. It was an exalted and tortuous period. Isaac was determined to serve his new "idols," love and literature, even if he found neither easy to satisfy. But at the same time, he proved to be fragile and prone to depression. It was as if the historical setting where he took his first steps as a writer—from Hitler's abortive Munich putsch to the Nuremberg racial laws—contributed to nourishing his self-doubt and his doubts about the Ashkenazi community, vaguely sensing the oncoming catastrophe. Once again, Singer seemed split in two:

> In some book or magazine, I had stumbled upon a phrase: "split personality," and I applied this diagnosis to myself. This was precisely what I was—cloven, torn, perhaps a single body with many souls each pulling in a different direction. I lived like a libertine yet I didn't cease praying to God and asking for His mercy. I broke every law of the Shulhan Arukh and at the same time I read cabala books and Hasidic volumes; I had spotted the weaknesses in the famous philosophers and great writers yet I wrote things that emerged naïve, awkward, amateurish. Now my potency was beyond belief—suddenly I became impotent. Some kind of enemy roosted within me or a dybbuk who spited me in every way and played cat-and-mouse with me.[2]

"'THE' SINGER IN THOSE DAYS WAS HIS BROTHER"

To an outside observer, Singer would appear to have had everything he wanted. Wasn't he well on his way, and splendidly so? For Warsaw's Jewish intellectuals, the *Literarische Bletter* was at the center of cultural life. Short stories, poems, theater reviews, authors' interviews—this weekly published contributions from the best Yiddish writers. Though Singer made fun of his proofreader's job, deep in the kitchen of literature, he had to admit that there was no better way of approaching this milieu that so fascinated him. While waiting to find a furnished room, he stayed with one of the *Literarische Bletter*'s editors, Melech Ravitch, with whom he shared his thoughts on man and progress. There he was, in direct contact with that literary world he called the "big world."[3] Could he wish for anything more?

This was also the period when, once again thanks to Joshua, he would fulfill another dream and step into the holiest of holies, the Warsaw Yiddish Writers' Club. This mythical place remained almost as important a focal point in his imagination as Krochmalna Street. Years later, in Wengen, Switzerland, where he spent many summers with his French translator and editor, Marie-Pierre Bay, and his first French publisher, André Bay, "every night after dinner Singer kept re-creating, almost inevitably, the Yiddish Writers' Club."[4] The club was located at No. 13 Tlomackie Street. Since Isaac was living hand to mouth—the *Bletter* needed prodding to pay him the few zlotys he was owed every month—the club became his refuge. The food was reasonably priced; on occasion the waitresses extended him credit; he could read the newspapers, play chess, and attend plays. The club was also an important center for international Yiddish culture. Every year banquets were held in honor of writers from New York, Berlin, Paris, or Buenos Aires. Debates on aesthetics and politics raged. Under the portrait of the great Peretz, members discussed and argued late into the night. Stalinists, Trotskyists, anarchists, Zionists, or supporters of Yiddishkeit, many of the authors preached a literature committed to improving the world.

Hence, in the early 1920s, everything was in place for Singer to make a successful debut into the world he so desired to be a part of. He had not yet published any personal writing, but he had started to collaborate with many other newspapers, including *Radio*, an evening paper, and *La Journée parisienne*, a Yiddish newspaper published in France. He began undertaking translations. He translated Thomas Mann into Yiddish, as well as Stefan Zweig, Erich Maria Remarque, several erotic novels, and the Norwegian writer Knut Hamsun, for whom his passion never waned.

"When *The Magic Mountain* came out in Poland everyone thought the translation was a masterpiece," Szulim Rozenberg recalls. "I didn't read it until the early 1930s. It was always checked out of the library. But my brother-in-law had bought a copy, so I read a copy at my sister's house. Finally, they agreed to lend it to me, as long as I washed my hands first. The book was considered a real treasure."[5]

However, Singer's excellent translations were not enough to make his name. "It wasn't until the thirties that people talked about him in Warsaw and knew who he was," notes Rozenberg. "Even today, the oldest Warsaw residents don't have vivid memories of him."[6]

"I remember running into him once during a reading at the Writers' Club," says Michal Friedman, a Yiddish translator born in Lithuania in 1913. "It must have been in 1933 or 1934, right before he left for the United States. I was a journalism student. I still picture him there, among other Yiddish writers. But it should be said that no one paid much attention to him in those days. 'The' Singer in those days was his brother."[7]

AN INCURABLE SENSUALIST

There was no doubt about it: in those days "the" Singer was Joshua. Garnering recognition for another Singer would be no small feat. But Isaac had a plan. He was thinking about what his first original writings should be. Above all, he had found his ultimate subject matter: "The endless variations and tensions peculiar to the relations between the sexes."[8] Women. From the first day in Joshua's studio, he knew that women would be at the heart of his work. He was convinced you couldn't write a novel without a love story and that everyone who had tried had failed. He wanted to talk about human passions in a new way without misrepresenting or filtering them. Too bad if he shocked his readers and reviewers.

His own experience offered the necessary inspiration. Starting in the 1920s, his love life provided him with ready-made material. In his autobiographical writings, *A Young Man in Search of Love, The Certificate, Lost in America*, the narrator—clearly Isaac himself—goes from one woman's arms to the next's. He tries to be faithful to Gina, a woman twice his age who introduces him to true sexual pleasure, but then rushes off to Stefa; he has a pleasurable fling with Sabina, the militant Communist, but doesn't reject the advances of Marila, the young Polish maid . . . How tempting it is to identify Singer with this incurable sensualist! His head spins every time he changes rooms and landlords, and the waltz almost becomes a game: "Those who rented rooms were nearly all women. I rang, they opened, and we contemplated each other. After a while they asked what I did and when I told them that I worked for a publication they were instantly won over. Our glances met and mutely asked: perhaps? I had become a connoisseur of faces, bosoms, shoulders, bellies, hips. I speculated how much pleasure these various parts could provide if it came to an intimacy."[9]

Sometimes he even rented two rooms at the same time! Pure folly for a young man with no resources, but a convenient folly for someone treading a delicate path between multiple lives. Singer's main character is usually torn among three women. In *A Young Man in Search of Love*, their names are Gina, Stefa, and Sabina; in *Lost in America*, Lena, Nesha, and Zosia. This triangular configuration (a woman at each juncture, the narrator at the center) recurs like a leitmotif in Singer's works. In *The Certificate*, David navigates among Sonia, an employee in a lingerie store; Minna, who needs him for a fictive marriage; and Edusha, whose intelligence and diplomas intimidate him yet who ends up yielding to him nevertheless. In *Enemies*, Herman Broder lives with Yadwiga, the peasant woman who has saved his life; is having an affair with Masha, who lives for his visits; and has to deal with the reappearance of his first wife, Tamara, who he thought had died in the Holocaust. In *Shadows on the Hudson*, Grein, the main character, shuttles among his wife, Leah; his old hysterical lover, Esther; and young Anna, who takes him away from his family without his fully realizing what is happening to him. There are many more examples.

But the Singer protagonist never glories in his conquests. He isn't conceited. On the contrary, he is softhearted and sentimental, neither domineering nor manipulative. He isn't calculating and doesn't really control events. He is swept up into the most inextricable complications, like someone who can't help it, or is driven by some sort of dybbuk. "The difference between Don Giovanni or Casanova and the Jewish womanizer is that the latter doesn't have the simplistic immoral and irreligious cynicism of the first two," notes Marc Saporta. "Quite the opposite, Singer's Hermans and Itcheles have a sense of responsibility at the root of all their difficulties. They try very hard not to cause anyone grief; from a certain perspective, 'what makes Singer run' is precisely his desire to attend to all his mistresses at once and not neglect his wife or disappoint any of these women—in fact, to provide for their moral, sentimental, financial and, of course, physical needs."[10]

In this regard Singer may have been a womanizer, but he was not a Don Juan. Besides, he didn't look the part. Skinny, with sunken cheeks and protruding ears, he had none of his brother Joshua's charisma. He wore cheap clothes, his tie was always crooked, his shoelaces were untied, and his trousers hung loose as if about to fall off. To make matters worse, he always had a cold. Was it his lively mind that captivated women? Was it the way he listened to them and understood them? Or was it his boyish, vulnerable side? Was Singer really the tireless skirt chaser he made himself out to be, or did he embellish the roster of his conquests? At the end of his life, when he was teaching creative writing at the University of Miami, he confided in Lester Goran, one of his translators, that he had had a total of about thirty lovers—nowhere near Don Giovanni's proverbial *mille tre*. But Singer stressed one point: "I've never had a woman who didn't come to me. Never in all my life. If she doesn't come to me, nothing happens. I would not know how to seduce a woman."[11]

A "BODY WITH MANY SOULS EACH PULLING IN A DIFFERENT DIRECTION"

Be that as it may, by 1926 his two idols had already fused into one. Isaac dreamed of writing a book in which he could depict his multiple romantic attachments without inhibition.

> The literary works, the novels, all concurred that a man could love just one woman at a time and vice versa. But I felt that they lied. Rather than literature denying men's laws, the laws had seized literature in a trap and kept it there. I frequently fantasized about writing a novel in which the hero was simultaneously in love with a number of women. Since the Orientals were allowed to practice polygamy and to maintain harems

(if they could afford it), the European could do the same. Monogamy was a law established by legislators, not by nature. But an artist had to be true to nature, human nature, at least in his descriptions, regardless of how wild, unjust, and insane it might be.[12]

Singer focused his investigations on this "single body with many souls each pulling in a different direction."[13] He never sought to give a new form to the novel. On the other hand, he had an intuition early on that there was something new in the idea that things could "act" upon a man rather than man acting upon them—the way a billiard ball can bounce in many directions with one shot. In *The Certificate*, Singer writes, "A new literature must arise . . . Though literature has always studied character, it has almost always ignored modern man's characterlessness."[14] Man without character. This could be Singer's counterpart to Musil's "man without qualities," a hero governed by forces whose logic escapes him, a plaything in the hands of women pulling him in opposite directions, events beyond his grasp, and a God obstinately and outrageously silent. Not a weak person, but one with sufficient self-doubt to risk surrendering to the chaos of the world.

Heaven knows, in 1926 chaos was at its peak. In May, strengthened by his victory over the Bolsheviks, Marshal Pilsudski took power in Warsaw. Taking advantage of the instability of the democratic government, he entered the capital with fourteen regiments and announced his intention to purify Poland by establishing a "moral dictatorship." For many, this military coup was a declaration of civil war. Outside Poland, the situation was no more heartening. An elderly Irish woman, Miss Gibson, fired on Mussolini, and the Fascist activists seized the occasion to ransack the headquarters of opposition newspapers. Il Duce declared ideological warfare, presenting fascism as the clear-cut, categorical, determined antithesis to the entire democratic world. In Weimar Germany, Hitler dominated the first congress of the National Socialist Party. He reviewed a procession of five thousand men, who hailed him with outstretched arms for the first time.

Singer escaped the draft. He was rejected because of weak lungs and because the Polish government, considering Jews to be dangerous leftists, cautiously limited their number in the army. What a relief! Even the thought of military service had terrified him. He who demanded "the right and the privilege to stay away from others"[15] now had time to fulfill his creative aspirations. In 1925, he had published his first short story in number 60 of *Literarische Bletter*. The story was called *"Oyf der elter"* ("In Old Age"). It begins on Krochmalna Street and ends in the shtetl, not far from Bilgoraj; late in life the protagonist, Reb Moyshe-Ber, after straying from his family, becomes the father of a little boy named Yitskhok (Isaac). Singer's first piece of writing is the story of a birth—the symbolism is clear. The following short story is titled *"Vayber,"* a no less emblematic title meaning "women" in Yiddish.

The reception of *"Oyf der elter"* foreshadowed Isaac's future problems with Yiddish-speaking readers. *Literarische Bletter*'s editor in chief, who promised to print the story in the journal, was outspoken about his reservations: "He said that the piece was too pessimistic, that it lacked problems, and that the story was negative and almost anti-Semitic. Why write about thieves and whores when there were so many decent Jewish men and devoted Jewish wives? If such a thing were translated into Polish and a gentile read it, he might conclude that all Jews were depraved. A Yiddish writer, my editor argued, was honor-bound to stress the good in our people, the lofty and sacred. He had to be an eloquent defender of the Jews, not their defamer."[16]

This was prescient criticism. Throughout his life, Singer would face these kinds of critiques from part of his Jewish readership. Such comments exasperated him immediately. Why did a story have to be optimistic? Why did a Yiddish writer have to be a defender of his people? Could a work whose sole aim was to conduct a dialogue with the anti-Semites have any artistic value?[17] It didn't matter; Isaac decided not to get discouraged. Besides, his editor must have believed in him, for he published his second short story, *"Vayber,"* that same year, in number 80 of *Literarische Bletter*. While the first story was mysteriously signed "Tse," now the name Isaac Bashevis appeared in print for the first time. This was the beginning of a long string of pseudonyms—among them Segal and Varshavsky, names Singer used for his journalistic articles and minor writings. "Bashevis," from that day on, was reserved for what he considered the highest form of his art. Derived from his mother's name, to which Isaac added a possessive ending, this pen name paid homage to the woman he so admired. But it was also a way of warning the reader: he was not to be confused with Israel Joshua. It was impossible for him to remain "Singer's little brother," or to continue living in his shadow. By joining the two last names, Isaac asserted both belonging and rejection. He was a Hasid (Singer) and a Mitnagged (Bathsheba). He was combining the two opposing currents that had infused his childhood—Pinchos Menahem's mysticism and Bathsheba's rationalism. He was blending tradition and autonomy, his roots and his uniqueness. Once again, he was both here and elsewhere, and he proclaimed this ubiquity.

In 1926 and 1927, Isaac continued to publish short stories or fragments, among them "*Eyniklekh*" ("The Little Children") and "*Mendel Bagreber*" ("Mendel the Gravedigger"), which came out in the *Warshawer Schriften*, as well as "*Verter oder Bilder*" ("Words or Images"), which appeared in the *Literarische Bletter*. In 1928, he published "*Afn oylm ha-toye*" ("In the World of Chaos") in *Di Yidishe Velt*, a story in which the hero is a corpse who travels around Poland without realizing he is dead.[18] His career was launched; he had found his language and his pen name. He was surrounded by women, all of whom lavished tender feelings on him. His two idols, love and literature, were eager to be worshipped by him. Could he dream of anything else?

A STRIKING DISILLUSIONMENT

Apparently he could. All his writings describing this period reveal a striking disillusionment, a feeling that bordered on despair, one that Singer found difficult to explain. Did he have a particularly acute sense of the artificiality of the merry roaring twenties? Did he despair in the late twenties at the thoughtlessness of his fellow human beings who had learned nothing from the war and continued dancing on tombs, to the steps of the fashionable Charleston and fox-trot? He was struck by the absurdity of the ideas around him. "I often heard people

say: I believe in Zionism, in socialism, in a better world, in the en-
durance of Jews, in the power of literature, in democracy, and in
many other beliefs. But on what did they base their faiths?" Singer
asked. He wasn't fooled by anything, not by any belief or ideology. He
had seen twenty million people perish in the war almost before his
eyes, "this one for Russia, that one for Germany, some for the Revolution, others for the Counter-Revolution, this one while capturing
some village, the other while retreating from the same village."[19] How
could he possibly still maintain his illusions?

History nourished his pessimism. The news from the Soviet Union
was terrifying. The Warsaw Trotskyite journals denounced the Sta-
linist abominations: hard labor camps, mock trials, the liquidation of
old Bolsheviks, purges . . . As communism gained ground, the situation of many Polish Jews was becoming increasingly precarious. In
The Certificate, an elderly man explains to David's father—who bears
a suspicious resemblance to Singer's own—how much the Jewish
Warsaw he used to know has changed in the last dozen years:

> On Krochmalna Street, where you used to be a rabbi, they've
> all become Communists. They say quite openly that if they
> achieve power, they'll kill all the cultivated Jews. Your son—
> my son-in-law—has just come from Russia. Ask him, he'll tell
> you. Here in the little towns where there are Bolsheviks, the
> blockheads have formed mobs to beat those Jews who are bour-
> geois. They've dragged householders off to Russia and who
> knows where else. They plucked out a rabbi's beard. In Russia
> itself things are dark indeed—human beings have no worth at
> all. The Gentiles launch pogroms, and the Jewish Communists
> torment religious Jews. They invade synagogues and steal the
> books to use as waste paper. They create all sorts of havoc.
> They've mounted up in their man-made heaven, where they've
> discovered there is no God. So what's to become of us all, eh? If
> God means to send the Messiah, what's taking him so long?[20]

Indeed, Singer's private war against the Almighty grew more bitter. Anti-Semitic acts of violence were multiplying everywhere. Men's

beards were cut off, fights broke out at night in the Saxony Gardens, people were insulted and publicly humiliated. On a train to Warsaw in 1923, Singer had already witnessed scare tactics of human degradation, when a bunch of hooligans abused men in caftans and forced them to sing the hymn celebrating the coming of the Sabbath. These kinds of incidents had now become everyday occurrences. The Jews were Bolsheviks, Trotskyites, Soviet spies, deicides, exploiters. The Polish government decided to bar them from municipal employment. At the university, Jewish enrollment was limited to 10 percent. Jewish students were required to sit separately from the others, on the left side of the classroom. Since many of them refused to submit to the rule, as a sign of protest they remained standing and took notes on the backs of their classmates.

Singer didn't claim to be a victim. The words he puts in Stefa's mouth in *A Young Man in Search of Love* could easily have been his own: "The Poles have had quite enough of us and I can see their side of it. We've lived here for eight hundred years and have remained strangers. Their God is not our God, their history is not our history. Most of us can't even speak a proper Polish. One time I watched a huge Zionist demonstration with blue and white flags and Stars of David and the whole falderal. They stopped the trolleys and shouted slogans in Hebrew and Yiddish. The gentiles stood around staring as if at a freak show."[21]

But the political climate was not the only problem. Isaac was in despair not just over the vagaries of history, God, the Christians, the Jews, or man in general, but also over his own identity. As early as 1923, he contemplated suicide, and from then on the idea was ever present in his mind. "At the onset of the 1930s," Singer wrote as the opening line to *Lost in America*, "my disillusionment with myself reached a stage in which I had lost all hope."[22] Self-doubt and doubts about the future were the reasons for his anguish. True, he had found his calling, but he had not yet made as big a name for himself as he had hoped. What had he published? Merely a handful of translations, articles, and short stories. He couldn't help comparing himself to Joshua. The worldly people in his brother's circle spoke perfect Polish and regarded "the young Singer" as a bit of a curiosity. Isaac wasn't really jealous. He hadn't forgotten how reliably Joshua had helped him since he was a child. But that was exactly the problem: he wanted to succeed without his brother's help and was annoyed at himself for not being able to. Intellectually, he felt he was as dependent as when he was twelve and his brother had given him the translation of *Crime and Punishment*. Financially, he was living hand to mouth. And he was proud—Genia had nicknamed him "the Starving Squire"[23]— preferring to go without food rather than ask for help. Yet, like an invisible hand, Joshua's presence always seemed to materialize at the crucial moment, as if anticipating Isaac's weaknesses, his needs, his torments.

In 1929, two events added to his anxiety: the death of his father and the birth of an unwanted child.

First was the demise of Pinchos Menahem. Isaac saw him a short time before he died. His father had been suffering from a stomach illness and had come to Warsaw to see a doctor. During that visit he had also tried to get his commentary on Rashi published. Isaac realized his father was much sicker than he had been led to believe. He even noticed that "his blue eyes reflected the ponderings of those whose time has come." His grief over his father's death was much greater than he had expected. More than forty years later, he wrote that he still could not "go into details about this loss."[24] His father's "saintliness," his unshakable faith in God, suddenly took on a dismaying importance in his mind. How many times had Pinchos Menahem urged him to behave like a good Jew? Isaac's response had been a lack of faith, womanizing, and a passion for writing. How many times had his father told him that secular writers "were a gang of clowns, lechers, scoundrels"? That it was "the greatest merit to write a book and to glorify the Torah"?[25] Isaac was overwhelmed by feelings of shame and futility, of betrayal and guilt. Whether he liked it or not, his father's death would remain a perpetual reproach.

"THOU SHALT NOT OVERLY PROCREATE"

One more reproach, that is. Isaac already reproached himself for a thousand things. In those years when elation and suffering went hand in hand, he felt guilty about his attitudes toward women. He knew "full well that playing around with women meant toying with lives," but he "lacked the character and the strength to heed the voice of [his] conscience."[26] He felt guilty for leading, in the eyes of his brother, a dissolute love life; he felt guilty for his fanatical individualism and his inability to contemplate a monogamous, lifelong relationship with anyone—particularly not through the institution of marriage! As it happened, many women wanted to marry him. Isaac did not always have the courage to turn them down. In Bilgoraj he had even promised to marry his cousin Esther, and then he left town and never contacted her again.

In his opinion, committing oneself to "a contract to love for an entire lifetime" was an absurdity: "I had read Otto Weininger's *Sex and Character* and had resolved never to marry. Weininger, Schopenhauer, Nietzsche, and my own experiences had transformed me into an antifeminist. I lusted after women yet at the same time I saw their faults, chief of which was that they (the modern, not the old-fashioned kind) were amazingly like me—just as lecherous, deceitful, egotistical, and eager for adventures."[27]

This seems to have been true of Rokhl Shapira, or Runya. Did this rabbi's daughter, educated in Polish schools, become Singer's legal wife or not? Accounts differ on this point. However, there is no denying that, in 1929, she gave birth to Singer's only child, Israel. Emancipated, Runya was the opposite of what Singer saw as his ideal wife, one who would have fulfilled his pious parents' dreams. What was she like? No doubt a combination of Sabina and Lena as they appear in *A Young Man in Search of Love* and *Lost in America*. Singer had met her three years earlier at the Writers' Club. Short, slightly plump, Runya was not a beauty, but she exuded vitality. Her passionate temperament had drawn her to communism, and she was active in the cause. Singer's preoccupations were very far from hers, and he probably felt distant from her in general:

> She was anything but my type . . . For me to associate with such a woman, and to become father of her child, was an act of madness. But I had already accustomed myself to my queer behavior. For some reason unknown to myself, this wild woman

evoked within me an exaggerated sense of compassion. Although she said at every opportunity that I need assume no responsibility for her and that I was free to do as my heart desired, she clung to me. She was a coil of contradictions. One day she swore eternal love to me. The next day she said that she wanted to become pregnant because the court would be inclined to be more lenient with a mother.[28]

It is easy to imagine that what he says here about Lena could well apply to Runya. But very little is known about her. Singer never mentions her explicitly in his autobiographical writings. Not once does he refer to her—or his son—in his conversations with Richard Burgin. Was he trying to protect or forget her? While they lived together, Runya was arrested several times for her political activities. In 1932, Singer also spent a day behind bars. There he was among thieves and Communists: he would always recall the dreadful feeling of humiliation. This arrest was the last straw. Their arguments, already frequent, reached a fever pitch. Isaac kept his distance. Monogamy was definitely not for him. The couple broke up for good in 1934. Years later, Singer remarked, unforgivingly, "We lived through eight miserable years."

But there was the child. Isaac as father seems implausible; he, of all people, whose revised and corrected version of the Ten Commandments included, "Thou shalt not overly procreate."[29] Having a child gave him a feeling of hopelessness and despair. True, he never expressed these feelings so bluntly, but, once again, they end up in the mouth of one of his characters—Asa Heshel, one of the heroes of *The Family Moskat*, whom Singer later said he greatly resembled. Asa Heshel frequently warns his wife, Adele, that if she were to get pregnant, he would run away and she would never hear from him. When it happens, Asa is terrified by the pregnancy and the responsibility he will have to assume. Little by little he feels himself becoming disconnected. Finally, when he meets his little son David, several years after his birth, he decides not to become attached to him for fear it would give Adele the power to blackmail him.

Clearly Singer experienced these same emotions. Clearly the accidental birth of his son added to the turmoil of his inner life. And to his feelings of shame—shame at shirking his responsibilities and, perhaps, at being over twenty-five and, like Asa Heshel, not having accomplished much. To combat this feeling, Isaac, too, ran away. Five years later, he abandoned both Runya and Israel. Twenty years passed before he saw his son again at Israel's request.

Singer's inner confusion in the mid-1930s was matched by the chaos overtaking Europe. Germany witnessed a National Socialist tidal wave. Poland gave birth to authoritarian regimes. Deep down, Polish Jews felt condemned. How could Singer abandon a five-year-old child? How could he leave him in Poland when he had a clear foreboding of what was going to happen? This is an enigma, never mentioned in any piece of writing, letter, or frank conversation of Singer's. Even people who had been close to him talk about it only in veiled terms, or gloss over it as if it were a minor detail. Minor, but taboo.

Ardor, passion, pride, shame, despair: These feelings formed a complex web of emotions that, in the early thirties, drove Singer to wonder if he wasn't mad. Or possessed by a dybbuk. He was prone to nightmares, and he combed through psychiatry books, including those of Freud, Jung, and Adler, in an attempt to understand why his moods could seesaw from depression to elation in a matter of seconds. Once again he felt divided, convinced that two Isaacs coexisted within him, one driven by ambition and the other depressive, seizing "every possible pleasure at any price" before vanishing.[30] Some scholars have described his work as "manic-depressive" as well, "at times carried by a vital jubilation, at times close to despair."[31] Note also that Isaac's first novel, *Shoten in Goray* (*Satan in Goray*), completed in Warsaw in 1933, is a story of madness on a vast scale, the account of a collective attack of religious hysteria that shook Poland in the mid-seventeenth century.

In 1933, madness stalked Isaac. The international press reported nothing but grim news: Hitler as chancellor of the Reich, the Reichstag fire, and the first concentration camp. That year both Thomas

Mann and Bertolt Brecht fled Germany. Joshua sensed the imminent danger as well. By then he was Warsaw correspondent for the American Yiddish newspaper the *Jewish Daily Forward*, and he accepted their offer to move to New York with his wife and youngest son, Joseph. He emigrated from Poland in 1933, leaving Isaac, who felt lonelier and more distraught than ever, behind. His father had died, without ever saying a word about his writings. His mother lived in Dzikow with his brother Moishe, who had become a rabbi. He had not seen either of them for ten years. His sister Hinde Esther lived in England with her son Maurice. His experience with Runya was a fiasco. In 1934, she tried to persuade him to move to the Soviet Union, but Singer wouldn't hear of it. He was convinced that the Eden she described was hell in disguise. However, he wasn't opposed to the idea of leaving Poland. On the contrary, the situation in Warsaw seemed less and less tolerable to him. So when Joshua invited him to come to America at the beginning of 1935, he made up his mind immediately and prepared to leave. He received his visa for the United States—practically a miracle. To obtain the precious stamp on his passport, with help from the Warsaw PEN Club, he had had to show he had a means of support in the United States. The frail redhead who lacked self-confidence and thought of himself as awkward and useless suddenly became bold before the official who asked him what he was planning to do in the United States. Surprised by his own composure, he replied that he was planning to write books, give lectures, and live like a celebrity!

Years later, Isaac said that when he uttered these words, he was convinced he was lying.

FIVE

"A Bare Soul"

CONVINCED HE WAS LYING: Is this really true? A great reader of
Spinoza, Singer knew that the truer a truth is, the more crippled it appears.[1] In fact, at thirty, his desire to write books and live like a
celebrity could not have been greater. But the prospect of exile, of extreme solitude, and the fear of failure filled him with a pessimism that
reached its peak in the late thirties. His despair—appropriate to the
times—and his ambition were in some sense intertwined. In the
spring of 1935, Singer was just a minor Yiddish writer with few
resources—a would-be writer, he later said. He was well aware of
this. Apart from his first novel, *Satan in Goray*, still in print when he
left Poland, he had published only a few short stories. Not only was he
overcome with self-doubt, but he was also suddenly afraid. Afraid of
failing at his grand literary goals. Afraid of his omnipresent feelings
of deep guilt. Afraid of the war and the inferno looming ahead. And
since he "didn't possess the courage to kill [himself]," his "only chance
to survive," frightening as well, "was to escape from Poland."[2]

    Singer packed his clothes and manuscripts in two suitcases. He
bade farewell to his entourage and prepared to leave Warsaw, knowing he would never return. He was leaving behind not only a country,
a city, and a culture, but also a woman, son, mother, brother, and
lovers, all of whom would soon be plunged into the recesses of memory. He realized that he was fleeing from danger at a time when those

left behind were facing the threat of pure evil. What was his state of mind? What words did he use to say goodbye to Runya and Israel, the little five-year-old his parents had nicknamed "Gigi" and who looked at him with uncomprehending blue eyes?

Seventy years later, little Gigi—whose real name is Israel Zamir (the Hebrew for Singer)—has become a journalist in Israel. He has hardly any memories of his early childhood in Warsaw. But he does remember the day in 1935 when his father, Isaac Singer, took him in his arms and kissed him: "He said to me: 'Gigi, I won't see you for a very long time. But be a good boy.' He was wearing a sleeveless gray pullover and his beard was prickly. My mother was there, too. He said he was going to join his brother in New York, and that later he would arrange for us to follow. For years, I harbored the notion that I had a father in America with whom I would soon be reunited."[3]

In theory, this idea wasn't so far-fetched. The historian Nancy Green writes that, at the time, "[t]he men left first. Then the women joined them, taking along all the household objects, a sign the family was resettling."[4] But what Runya and Israel didn't know was that Singer's visa to the United States was only a six-month tourist visa. How could he arrange to bring anyone over? In fact, mother and son soon realized they had taken his words much too literally; Isaac had no intention of having them join him. A short time later, they too escaped from Poland. They went to Palestine, via the Soviet Union and Turkey, in the late 1930s. Israel Zamir describes "their desolate lives in cheap hotels in Istanbul, without passports, without money in their pockets, their terror at every policeman, every knock on the door."[5] Up until 1940, Runya wrote to Isaac, probably through Joshua, asking him for money. But he never sent any. He couldn't. He was scarcely supporting himself. Time passed. Israel and Runya vanished completely from his world.

FIFTY DOLLARS IN HIS POCKET

Was Isaac sincere when he left? Had he knowingly lied to Runya and Israel by promising to see them again on the other side of the Atlantic? If so, could he foresee the hardships awaiting this woman and her child? It seems doubtful. Later, in a short story titled "The Son," he wrote the following words, so revealing of his "family feeling"— and his need to justify himself after the fact: "What is a son after all? What makes my semen more to me than somebody else's? What value is there in a flesh-and-blood connection? We are all foam from the same caldron."[6]

This probably explains why neither Runya nor Israel was at the station to see him off on April 19, 1935. Isaac did not want them there. Their presence would merely have deepened his anxiety about his forthcoming trip. The journey ahead seemed long and perilous. The first Paris–New York flight had been celebrated five years earlier, but, of course, Singer would be crossing the Atlantic by ship. He had to travel to Paris by train, with the equivalent of fifty dollars in his pocket, not a penny more, and then to Cherbourg, where he would board the French ship *Champlain*. First he had to cross Germany, in the midst of rearmament in April 1935. Though it was six months before the race laws were presented before the Nazi Party Congress, persecution against the Jews had already started. Germany had seven concentration camps controlled by special "Death's-Head units," so called because of the skull-and-bone insignia the guards wore in Dachau starting in late 1933. Singer confronted the very real danger of being arrested and sent to a concentration camp.

He reached the border; passports were checked. Two men wearing swastikas quizzed him briefly, exchanged a "Heil Hitler!" and left. Isaac was relieved but puzzled: Why had the Nazis been so uninquisitive? He looked out the window: All the balconies were decorated with Nazi banners. It was April 20, 1935, and Germany was celebrating the führer's forty-sixth birthday. Isaac had unwittingly benefited from the festive atmosphere of the national holiday. But in Berlin, he had another scare on the train. A young man came into his car and called out his name. Singer thought he was about to be arrested, but the young man turned out to be a Pole who had heard of him and had come to give him some Passover delicacies. Isaac was truly lucky. After thirty-six hours, a conductor tapped him on the shoulder. He had arrived in Paris at last. The Yiddish Writers' Club had given him the address of a cheap hotel in Belleville, where he planned to stay for two or three nights before taking the train to Cherbourg. Isaac settled into a garret with a brass bed and a sink. He developed an immediate affection for the city.

Paris. Spring 1935. It was a time of turmoil and confusion. The failure of the Stresa conference and the powerlessness of France's national defense forces in the face of German rearmament dominated the newspaper headlines. The press denounced Adolf Hitler's two-faced speech: "Does Hitler's Germany want peace, as the Chancellor solemnly proclaims today, or does the country want war—the war to which this same Chancellor kept exhorting it before he attained supreme power?"[7] The chaos in France was just as great in the world of ideas. Claiming to defend a "new conception of human progress," the Nobel laureate Alexis Carrel was putting the finishing touches on *Man the Unknown*, a work that, according to *Le Figaro* at the time, "addresses itself to all those who wish to escape from the enslaving dogmas of modern civilization!" Pierre Drieu La Rochelle, who received a prize for his *Comédie de Charleroi*, was described by Julien Benda as "a fascist with a socialist heart," while Louis Aragon's first "politically committed novel," *The Bells of Basel*, published several months earlier, was being discussed in literary circles.

Singer was unaware of these debates and of the Montparnasse circle of writers and artists described by another foreigner, Henry Miller, in *Tropic of Cancer*. Just as he had remained outside non-Jewish literary Warsaw—for instance, he never mentioned Polish writers of his generation, such as Witold Gombrowicz, born the same year he was—it is likely he had never heard of André Breton, Paul Eluard, Michel Leiris, Surrealism, or any of the French avant-garde movements flourishing at the time. He had probably never heard of the École de Paris, although most of the artists were Jewish. Isaac was an outsider to all this, but what did that matter? After his trying journey, he surrendered to the peaceful atmosphere. It was a warm spring that year. Maurice Chevalier was the hit of the Casino de Paris. Parisians were humming the melodies of Tino Rossi and Ray Ventura. The whole country sang, *"Tout va très bien, madame la marquise"* (Everything's fine, madame marquise), a song prescient and ironic. Singer was enchanted. He discovered Belleville, one of the Jewish immigrants' favorite haunts. Some of the stores had signs in their windows warning, "The sales representatives of German firms are no longer welcome." The slogan was illustrated with a swastika made of intertwining snakes in a birdcage. The chicken noodle soup in the restaurants had the same smell as in Warsaw, Vilna, and Gdansk. The main subject of conversation was the peace conference the Communists were planning to convene. One evening Singer attended a performance of *Yoshe Kalb*, a play adapted from his brother Joshua's novel.

THE ISLAND OF TEARS

Nevertheless, Singer was still eager to leave France. His press card—a document issued by the *Pariser Haint* (The Parisian Day), a daily on the rue du Faubourg du Temple to which he had sometimes contributed from Warsaw—was issued to "Icek Hersz Zynger (pseudonym I. Baszewis)," a "special correspondent" for the paper. Photographic identification shows a young man, almost bald, peering through thick dark glasses—a man on the run. This was partly true. To buy himself some time, he had turned down the opportunity to travel—in the cheapest class—on the *Normandie*, scheduled to make her maiden transatlantic voyage two weeks later, in a record four days.[8] Instead he chose to sail on the *Champlain*, in a cabin without portholes. Paris had been fleeting but tranquil. As he set off for Cherbourg, Singer was filled with anxiety. On the deck of the ship his anxiety intensified, mixed with loneliness, fear of having to share his cabin with a stranger, nervousness at traveling with no money, and great apprehension, understandable, in anticipation of the symbolic moment when the ship would leave the shores of the Old World for good.

"They took my ticket, and my pockets felt empty. All I had there now was my passport. I had been left practically penniless . . . My two valises stood in the dark cabin, silent witnesses that I had lived nearly thirty years in Poland . . . I was what the cabala calls a naked soul—a soul which has departed one body and awaits another."[9]

The crossing lasted a week. For five days, Singer spoke to no one. He even asked that his meals be served in his cabin. He left for America like a prison recluse, engrossed in reading Bergson's *Creative Evolution* in German. The antisocial "mocking demon"[10] clung to him, isolating him from the rest of the world, a society of young people in knickers playing badminton on deck or standing in line for the evening concert—a world that wasn't his.

This man who was shedding all ties looked like an immigrant, like all those who arrived at America's doorstep by the thousands, their hearts torn between hope and fear. When he lifted his eyes from his book, he tried to imagine Ellis Island, known as the "island of tears." He visualized the foreigners from all parts of the world who disembarked there every day, like those described by Henry Roth in *Call It Sleep*, "the joweled close-cropped Teuton, the full-bearded Russian, the scraggly-whiskered Jew, and among them Slovack peasants with docile faces, smooth-cheeked and swarthy Armenians, pimply Greeks, Danes with wrinkled eyelids."[11] He could almost hear the commotion as people watched over their children and baggage and waited for the terrifying medical examination. He could guess the immigration officers' questions, to which some immigrants memorized the answers for fear of being turned back.

In the 1930s, Jews continued to flock to America from all parts of Eastern Europe. What did they find on Ellis Island, that Tower of Babel where the walls were covered with notices in a dozen languages? A canteen, dormitories, a hospital, interpreters, a window where they went to get their names Americanized. First, they were made to sit on wooden benches, along the metal guardrails of the great registration hall. There they waited, under the Star-Spangled Banner, until they were called and questioned. "Where do you come from? Where are you going? Are you a prisoner, polygamist, or prostitute?" Then they were put in the care of services designed to help and orient them.

"At Ellis Island there was an office for changing money, a window for buying domestic train tickets, a telegraph bureau, several restaurants, and a hairdresser. There were also many volunteer agencies to protect immigrants from all kinds of swindlers, including ubiquitous hotel and boardinghouse agents who were often far from scrupulous.

It wasn't infrequent for an immigrant to think he had purchased a train ticket to Boston when he had actually purchased a subway ticket to the Bronx."[12]

A CULTURE IN FULL BLOOM

For Jewish immigrants, New York was usually the end of the journey. In 1935, the year Singer arrived, the city counted 3.5 million Yiddish speakers, many of whom lived in the Lower East Side, forming the largest Yiddish-speaking community in the world. The culture was thriving. People thronged to the theaters, where each performance—a mixture of "commedia dell'arte, cabaret, and people's university"— was an event.[13] The Jewish Art Theater, in particular, booked all the great names in Yiddish literature; people were as entranced by what was going on in the audience as they were with the onstage performance. Poetry also played an important role: many proletarian poets depicted the poverty of the sweatshops, and workers at their sewing machines sang poems more like anarchist slogans than poetic verses. It was the golden age of the Yiddish press, with publications including *Tageblatt*, *Tsukunft*, *Yiddisher Kemfer*, and *Abend Blatt*. The *Jewish Daily Forward* (*Forverts* in Yiddish), where Joshua worked, was a Lower East Side institution. Created by a group of Socialists in 1897 in the hope of destroying the dominance of *Tageblatt* (considered too reactionary), the *Forward* was a Social Democratic daily with a progressive orientation and a wide readership. At its peak it had a circulation of 250,000 and eleven local or regional editions. Abraham Cahan, the paper's editor in chief, was a legendary figure, a strong, energetic man overflowing with ideas. He was also a writer, which no doubt explains the originality of his newspaper. The *Forward* offered its readers practical advice in every issue, such as addresses for courses in English and daily Letters to the Editor (*Bintel brief*), a fascinating mirror of immigration. But above all, the *Forward* welcomed the important writers of the day—Z. Shneour, S. Asch, A. Reizen, J. Rosenfeld—who contributed opinion pieces and literary texts. It was through the *Forward* that most of the Yiddish poets and writers made a name for themselves. Since publishing houses were rare (the readership was limited and the investment too great), it was the Yiddish press, to quote Rachel Ertel, that "gave birth" to literature at the time.[14]

LOST IN AMERICA

The mythical *Forward* was among the first things Singer saw upon his arrival in New York. Joshua came to meet him at the ship and brought along one of his friends, the writer Zygmunt Salkin. Such reunions were usually heartening moments for immigrants. Henry Roth describes it best: "The most volatile races, such as the Italians, often danced for joy, whirled each other around, pirouetted in an ecstasy: Swedes sometimes just looked at each other, breathing through open mouths like a panting dog; Jews wept, jabbered, almost put each other's eyes out with the recklessness of their darting gestures . . . and after one pecking kiss, the English might be seen gravitating toward, but never achieving an embrace."[15]

Isaac and Joshua didn't fit any of these descriptions. There was no euphoria in their reunion; quite the opposite. A sense of propriety—or distance—reigned. In his writings, Singer completely expunged the emotional side of the moment, as though the person who had come to pick him up were a random taxi driver. Isaac hadn't seen his brother for two years, yet he managed to slip in a few harsh comments, noting that Joshua "seemed to have aged" and that "the hair surrounding his bald skull had grown nearly grey." Isaac's ambivalent feelings are strange. By making him come to America, arranging for his passport and visa, Joshua had saved his life. Isaac was grateful to him but also resented him—much as the proud might come to hate those to whom they are indebted. At the same time, he reproached himself for his ingratitude. He was ill at ease. This comes out in Singer's response to his brother's comments on the day of his arrival:

> [Joshua] critically considered my wide suspenders and jokingly remarked that I resembled a Western sheriff. He said, "Well, you're in America and one way or another you'll stay here.

Your tourist visa will be extended for a year or two and I'll do everything possible to keep you from going back. All hell will break out over there. Should you meet a girl who was born here, and should she appeal to you enough to marry, you'll get a permanent visa on the spot."

I blushed. In the presence of my brother, I had remained a shy little boy.[16]

This was the shy little boy who got his first tour of New York on May Day, 1935, in the rear of Zygmunt Salkin's car. The els; Fifth and Madison avenues, Riverside Drive, Wall Street; suspension bridges, a tangle of iron and steel, chrome and marble lobbies: New York impressed him "as a giant exhibition of Cubist paintings and theater props."[17] A great construction game, angular, gleaming, surreal. After two hours of immersion in modernity, Isaac stopped in front of the ten-story *Jewish Daily Forward* building, where his brother had an office. The *Forward* was not just a landmark in the life of New York Jews. It was also an institution that established writers' reputations. Isaac was moved at the sight but could never have imagined the decisive role the *Forward* would play in his life. That day, the columns of the building were draped in red; a large crowd was assembled in front of the entrance listening to the May Day speeches. "I thought, such a thing would have been unthinkable in Poland."[18]

They crossed the Brooklyn Bridge and drove out to Coney Island and Seagate, where Joshua and his family were staying for the summer. Singer was exhausted, physically and mentally. But he was also amazed. An amusement park burst into the landscape. Isaac had never seen anything like it. America, with its speed, its loud noises and insouciance, suddenly looked to him like a vision of the apocalypse:

To the left, the ocean flashed and flared with a blend of water and fire. To the right, carrousels whirled, youth shot at tin ducks. On rails emerging from a tunnel, then looming straight up into the pale blue sky, boys rode metal horses while girls sitting behind them shrieked. Jazz music throbbed, whistled, screeched. A mechanical man, a robot, laughed hollowly. Before a kind of museum, a black giant cavorted with a midget on each arm. I could feel that some mental catastrophe was taking place here, some mutation for which there was no name in my vocabulary, not even a beginning of a notion.[19]

Singer was speechless before this unfathomable world and remained so for several years. For the time being, Joshua had rented an additional room for him in the house where he, his wife, Genia, and their son Joseph were living. Years later, Joseph would describe his first impression of his uncle Isaac: shy, uncommunicative, withdrawn. Joshua was as gregarious and outgoing as Isaac was reserved and introverted. In later years Joseph said he was always surprised when he saw his uncle give a public reading. He couldn't believe it was the same man he had known as so bashful and inhibited.[20]

In Seagate, Singer sank into an even greater state of depression. He had never given much thought to his height, but he suddenly felt short compared to these American giants, the suntanned athletic Goliaths whose healthful glow contrasted so acutely with his sickly pallor. What was most distressing was that Isaac felt detached from himself. He had no desire for anything: reading bored him; the notes he had jotted down for short stories left him cold. A deep gloom came over him. He spent his days lying on his bed, demoralized, with no urge to write, turning dark thoughts over in his head.

"I was still young . . . but I was overcome by a fatigue that most probably comes with old age. I had cut off whatever roots I had in Poland yet I knew that I would remain a stranger here to my last day. I tried to imagine myself in Hitler's Dachau, or in a labor camp in Siberia. Nothing was left for me in the future."[21]

Soon he felt tempted to commit suicide again: "A rage filled me against America, against my brother for bringing me here, and against myself and my accursed nature. The enemy reposing within me had scored a smashing victory. In my anxiety I resolved to book a return trip to Poland as quickly as possible and to jump overboard en route there."[22]

———

Isaac was a bundle of contradictions. One day, he wanted to commit suicide; the next day, he vowed to get his visa extended at all costs. Time passed; he did nothing. Joshua, sensing the intensity of his melancholy, looked after him. He took him to Manhattan and forced him to exchange his heavy black Polish suit for a lightweight American one. He worked behind the scenes so his brother wouldn't remain inactive, arranging for the *Forward* to commission articles from him. But nothing helped. Even women failed to distract him. As was his habit, Isaac surrounded himself with admiring women who tried to ease his suffering. He became attached to a widow, older than he, who rented rooms in Seagate; she made him discard his stiff collar and hat when he strolled down the boardwalk. He went out, to the movies and the Yiddish theater, and took English lessons. He tried to take his mind off things by moving to new lodgings several times. But these were mere stopgap solutions. In those two dark years, 1935 and 1936, his melancholy was such that he felt empty and impotent. His "inner I," or "superego" as he called it, suffered from his brother's example. Success came easily to Joshua. He liked America, its freedom and tolerance. He had interesting work, a devoted wife, a son of bar mitzvah age. He had friends, he entertained at home, he seemed at ease. And, above all, he had just finished his third novel, *The Brothers Ashkenazi*. With this book—written in Yiddish but translated into English and published by Knopf—Joshua was well on the way to becoming a bestselling writer. Indeed, in 1936, *The Brothers Ashkenazi* was at the top of the bestseller list, along with *Gone With the Wind*. Here too, Isaac couldn't help but compare himself to the man he sometimes called his "master." He hadn't even received a printed copy of his first novel and felt he had truly reached an impasse.

"It seemed that I had a great talent for suffering . . . The skeptic in me, the nihilist and protester, quoted the words of Ecclesiastes: 'Of laughter I said it is madness and of mirth what doeth it?' I was still a Yiddish writer who hadn't made it, estranged from everything and everybody. I could live neither with God nor without him. I had no faith in the institution of marriage, neither could I stand my bachelor's loneliness."[23]

Ensnared in these tensions, depressed, and dissatisfied with himself, Singer sank into a period of creative sterility from which he feared he would never recover.

LOVE AT FIRST SIGHT IN THE CATSKILLS

Between 1937 and 1943, however, three important events took place. Though they didn't immediately give Singer the desire to write again, they laid the foundation for what later became his American life.

The first event was meeting Alma. Singer, who didn't believe in marriage, would have been surprised if he had been told, in 1937, that he would meet a woman he would marry three years later. He was spending that summer in Mountaindale, in the Catskills. Joshua and Genia had urged him to get away from the city. As improbable as it may seem, he had decided to spend the summer on a kind of farm that welcomed vacationing families. Room and board were not expensive—twelve dollars a week—and the place was liked by many émigrés. There was an artists' colony, Green Fields, a short distance away, and Joshua had rented a room in the vicinity.

Singer met Alma Haimann Wassermann in Mountaindale in the summer of 1937. Who would have wagered that this dark, refined, elegant woman would become his wife? At the time, Alma was married and a mother. She was different from Isaac in every respect. Of Jewish descent, Alma had been born in Germany to a well-to-do, completely assimilated mercantile family. Her father, a wealthy wholesaler and retailer in silk and velvet, divided his business activity between Munich and Milan. Her mother was the sole heir of an important men's clothing manufacturer in Munich and Nuremberg. In the 1910s, while Isaac was attending heder and braving the poverty of Krochmalna Street, Alma was receiving a comfortable bourgeois education. There was no trace of Yiddishkeit in her education. The young girl had no knowledge of the language. She studied English and literature. Later, she learned to dance and took great pride in her appearance. She liked going out to *thés dansants* in the big hotels of Geneva, where part of her family lived. She spent several months in Switzerland after graduating from high school in Germany. In the twenties, while Singer was living hand to mouth in Warsaw, Alma was in Munich. Her father had found her a job in a bank, where she seemed to be biding her time, waiting for the right suitor to appear. Very soon, she met a young chemist, Walter Wassermann, whom she married in 1927 and with whom she had two children, Inge and Klaus.

When they met in Mountaindale, Isaac and Alma were both recent immigrants. Alma had left Germany in the summer of 1936 and, like Isaac, never saw her parents again. The Wassermanns settled in Washington Heights, where many German Jewish immigrants lived at the time. That year, 1937, they had decided to spend their summer vacation in the Catskills, on the advice of their neighbors.

Fifty years later, Alma described her meeting with Isaac this way:

> It was as primitive as a place can only be. But nature was beautiful . . . The farmer's wife was not a good cook, so an old man took over and it was mostly a thrown together hodge-podge. But nobody complained. There were a few families with children there, many visitors as well and nearby was an artists' colony of Jewish writers and poets.
>
> Into this milieu stepped one evening a man who was also recommended to this farm. He was young, slim, blond, almost bald, had very blue eyes and seemed completely lost or disoriented as far as finding the dining room, his room or even the road outside, into the village or away from the village . . . We learned that he was a budding writer, that he had so far written one book and that it was a good book. This man was Isaac Bashevis Singer.[24]

Long walks in the forest, endless conversations . . . Alma got to know Isaac and fell under his spell, so much so that their relationship continued in New York in the fall of 1937.

> He told me he sometimes worked in the Public Library on 42nd Street, in the room of uneven numbers, and so one day I

went there to look for him without any previous appointment, and believe it or not, there he was sitting . . . Then we took walks, and from a friendship it developed into a romance and it got to the point where I just felt that I had to spend the rest of my life with him and therefore I had to give up my marriage and my children which was a very difficult and, really, a very terrible decision to make. But sometimes you have to do things and I never regretted it.[25]

Oddly enough, in his autobiographical writings, Isaac doesn't mention his meeting with Alma. Did he fall in love at first sight as well? Did he let things follow their course, as he usually did? Or was his marriage a coldhearted calculation? Here, there are divergent views. Based on a piece titled "Fun der alter un nayer heym" ("From the Old and New Home"), Janet Hadda—one of Singer's American biographers—believes she recognizes Alma in the character of Louisa. Hadda suggests that at the beginning of the relationship, Isaac was much more aloof than Alma. And he may even have cynically gone into it knowing it would be useful to his writing career.[26] Marie-Pierre Bay doesn't share this opinion at all, having heard accounts of the Mountaindale meeting several times from the protagonists themselves. As Bay tells it, one night in the Catskills, Alma had had the audacity to slip a note into Isaac's briefcase. Though they scarcely knew each other, Isaac read the following three words on the folded piece of paper: "I love you." Years later, says Marie-Pierre Bay, they both still blushed when they talked about it.[27]

In Singer's case, these two versions are not mutually exclusive. Whatever the case, in 1939, two years after this vacation, Alma finally obtained a divorce. She turned down all her husband's attempts at reconciliation and even gave him custody of their two children. She was free. Several months later, on February 14, 1940, in the midst of a blinding snowstorm, Singer and Alma were married at Borough Hall in Brooklyn. It was a ceremony without witnesses, completely private. In fact, Isaac even "forgot" to tell Runya and Israel.

The second key event occurred in 1942: Isaac was hired by the *Forward* as a permanent staff writer. This was an important triumph for him. Until then, he had lived off irregular freelance articles, sending his pieces in by mail and living in daily fear that his column might be eliminated. He lacked self-confidence, as always, and when he stopped by the newspaper, it was always at night so he wouldn't run into anyone. Above all, he wondered whether he owed his commissioned articles to his own merits or to his brother's intervention. Now he felt reassured. His column, "It's Worth Knowing," consisted of a selection of little social facts culled from the English-language press. Singer had a particular affinity for psychological subjects, ranging from crimes of passion to platonic love. But he was well aware this was just a job to pay the rent. He signed the column with a pseudonym, Yitskhok Varshavsky, "the man from Warsaw."

The third event was a bureaucratic success. In 1943, after six years of maneuvering, including a trip to Canada, Singer obtained American citizenship. Now he was finally in possession of legitimate papers, on a continent where Hitler and Stalin were no longer a threat. Now he could breathe.

BETWEEN A DEAD PAST AND AN IMPOSSIBLE FUTURE

In 1943, after eight years of deep malaise and inertia, Singer had created a solid foundation for himself. He had a wife, work, and papers. He was even beginning to speak English. Yet none of this had any effect on his emotional state. He still suffered from an insidious, oppressive writer's block. Ashamed, he hid even from Joshua, fearing that his brother would ask him about his writing. He threw a botched novel into the garbage, as well as the adaptation of a play that would never be performed. He reread his notes tirelessly, but to no avail. His paralysis even included his correspondence: "Somehow, I have a block about writing letters. It's even a burden for me to write to my mother. I make solemn vows to write the very next day, but when tomorrow comes, I forget all about it, or I make myself forget. As soon as I remind myself to write, I become as if paralyzed. This is a kind of madness, or the devil knows what."

Paralyzed. The news from Europe was increasingly traumatic. On the radio and in the newspapers, the headlines were horrifying. The descriptions of Poland under the Germans were particularly dispiriting for all Eastern European exiles. The press described executions in public squares, the systematic elimination of the Polish elite, rampant savagery.

"These executions are carried out by Gestapo agents and members of the S.S. with incredible refinements of cruelty," wrote *L'Illustration* in January 1940. "In Bydgoszcz, by the end of December 1939, over six thousand Polish men and women massacred, including 136 schoolboys aged twelve or thirteen." A lengthy enumeration of horror scenes follows, in Posnania, Pomerania, Silesia . . .

> Often people are arrested at home and taken to an unknown destination to work on agricultural hard labor inside the Reich. Entire families are uprooted this way, with children and parents. Then husbands and wives are carefully separated . . . As might be expected, the Polish language was immediately banned from public life, and in many places, it is even prohibited to use it in private conversation. All the Polish signs have been removed. The roads and squares bear German names. All the Polish newspapers have been suspended; the museums and theaters . . . have been requisitioned; Polish companies have been dissolved and their capital confiscated; schools have been Germanized and punishment by flogging has been reinstated.

The newspaper reported on the siege of Warsaw in the same issue. Cold, famine, terror:

> Horses killed in the streets were immediately dismembered for food. On September 23 [1939], a massive raid by the German air force destroyed the electric cables, the gas and water pipes, and the radio station . . . German planes, flying very low, machine-gunned everyone looking for food and water, attempting to put out fires or picking up the wounded. The dead were buried on the spot in the public gardens or squares. The worst day was September 25 . . . Sixty-five of the most beautiful

buildings in the city were reduced to rubble within twenty-four hours. Entire streets ceased to exist. Among the workers assigned the task of cleaning the streets under the supervision of German soldiers were former ministers, deputies, businessmen, and intellectuals, most of them elderly men. They work twelve hours a day; in the evening they are allowed to buy a bowl of soup at the German canteen at the cost of one zloty—six francs!—a ration.

At last, the martyrdom of the Polish Jewish population became public knowledge. In January 1940, the newspaper reported that three million Jews were waiting to be transferred to the Lublin *reservat*.

The transportation of the Jews destined to inhabit this huge penal colony is implemented in stages. After having imprisoned the 1,500,000 Polish Jews in the reservat, they will be sending 180,000 Bohemian and Moravian Jews there, followed by 65,000 from Vienna, 30,000 from Posnania (incorporated into the Reich), and finally 200,000 from Germany proper. The fate of the rest will be determined later." The newspaper concluded: "These are some of the characteristics of Polish life under the German heel . . . These kinds of methods recall a savagery that we might have thought banned forever in modern times and which should provoke the condemnation of the entire civilized world.[28]

In 1942, the news from Warsaw was even more terrifying. According to rumor, the deportations organized by the Germans had been stepped up. In the ghettos, the Jews were kept in atrocious sanitary conditions. In the extermination camps Chelmo, Majdanek, Sobibor, and Treblinka, thousands were gassed on arrival. What could remain of Krochmalna Street? In August it was reported that the Nazi authorities decided to close down Janus Korczak's children's house. The children, all of them Jewish, were deported to Treblinka. The Germans told Dr. Korczak he could stay in Warsaw, but not wanting to abandon his children, he decided to go with them to the gas chamber.

May 1943. After four weeks of fighting, the ghetto resistance ended. The few remaining survivors tried to escape through the sewers. General Stroop of the S.S. let it be known that his units had exterminated 56,065 Jews, including those who had chosen to burn with their houses. All that was left of the old Jewish city of Warsaw was rubble. Singer was shattered by the news. But the final blow came in 1944 when he learned of the death of his mother and younger brother. Bathsheba and Moishe were deported in a cattle car and taken from Dzikow to Russia. They died in Kazakhstan, under unknown circumstances, possibly simply of hunger and thirst. For Isaac, the pain was hard to bear. To make matters far worse, he hadn't written to them once since his departure from Warsaw.

Singer had never been as miserable in his life. Though Alma provided comfort, he had never felt so alone. His family, his culture, his past had been annihilated; he seemed incapable of adapting to life. He found it impossible to find inspiration in this new environment and had written almost nothing in eight years. In 1943, he had put his energies into getting his first novel, *Satan in Goray*, reissued and had published a few short stories. These were minor accomplishments. He was haunted by his powerlessness and felt his language was inadequate. As on the ship crossing the Atlantic, he was still a "bare soul," a shadow wandering between the two shores of his life—between a dead past and an impossible future.

SIX

"The Language of No One"

PARADOXICALLY, it was an unexpected death that breathed new life into Isaac. It took a real shock to shake him out of the depression that had consumed him for more than eight years. On the morning of February 10, 1944, Israel Joshua, after a dinner at Isaac and Alma's the night before, was suddenly felled by a heart attack. At fifty-one, he left his wife, Genia, who had never recovered from the death of the couple's first child, and a son, Joseph, who later became one of his father's and uncle's translators.

Joshua died of a heart attack. What contributed to this tragedy? The year 1944 witnessed the traumatic disclosures of the Holocaust. The American press had been reporting on the Nazi atrocities for more than a year. In August 1942, *Newsweek* reported that convoys crammed with Jews from Warsaw were vanishing into oblivion. In November of the same year, *The New York Times* published a news item from the Polish government in exile describing the camps of Sobibor and Treblinka. The newspaper referred to the gas chambers and crematoriums of Auschwitz. Rabbi Stephen Wise, a prominent American Jewish leader, was quoted as saying that the corpses were used to make fat for soap and lubricants.[1]

Nevertheless, for a long time, most Americans failed to grasp the scope of the tragedy. "The process of destruction was observed mainly in segments," writes the historian Raul Hilberg, who notes that "the

Jews had not created a central intelligence apparatus of their own. As passive recipients of data they did not build upon knowledge or study documents for clues to larger facts. Hence each new communication came to them as a surprise, even as late as 1944."[2]

Such was the case for the Singer brothers. Throughout the war, they received horrifying pieces of news from Poland, one after the other. "A day didn't go by that I didn't learn of the deaths and all kinds of tragedies suffered by people who had been known or been close to me,"[3] said Isaac. And yet, like the others, Isaac and his brother grasped the planned nature of the genocide only gradually. By 1944, it was impossible not to face the reality—the unimaginable reality—of the Final Solution. Joshua did not live to apprehend it. He passed away two months before the first Allied plane flew above Auschwitz and six months before the first bombing of the camp. Joshua died at the peak of his own success. In a mere ten years, this freethinking, strong-willed man, attracted by all the avant-garde movements, had managed to make a name for himself in the United States. Thanks to his novels (*The Brothers Ashkenazi*; *Yoshe Kalb*, adapted for the stage and first performed by the Yiddish Art Theater in 1933), he had become recognized as a writer. With time, his style had become more graceful. He had shed the weight of ideology in his writing, so much so that shortly before his death, his name was mentioned as a possible Nobel candidate.[4] Thirty-four years later, when Isaac received the award, he made sure to give Joshua due recognition. He praised his older brother's talent in countless interviews. Isaac talked about his brother as his "teacher of literature," someone who made him "grow." Years later, he said "his death caused me great anguish which has never healed."[5]

ANGUISH . . . AND LIBERATION

The sincerity of his grief is unquestionable. Yet, in spite of Isaac's protests, Joshua's death was also liberating for him. He seemed fated never to achieve anything as long as he lived in the shadow of his successful older brother. The unflagging help and attention Joshua lavished on him seemed merely to have added to his inhibitions and feelings of inferiority. The way Isaac spoke of Joshua in the early 1940s reveals the psychological impediment his brother represented for him. He loomed large in Isaac's mind, paralyzing him. Isaac lived in constant fear of not measuring up to Joshua's expectations. He avoided his gaze and feared his judgment. "I could never address him first. I always had to wait for him to make the first overture," he admits.[6] This detail is illustrative of the strange relationship that united the two brothers. Isaac's feelings for Joshua were a mixture of admiration and terror, reverence and fear. This complex mixture killed artistic spontaneity. How could he possibly create under his brother's watchful eye?

He felt he had to protect himself, to keep his distance. This was why, after his arrival in the United States, for his own peace of mind, Isaac moved to another part of the city. In 1936, he preferred to live alone in a seedy rented room on Nineteenth Street rather than continue living in Seagate. Later, he claimed he had lost Joshua's telephone number, an excellent excuse for avoiding him. Distance didn't quite solve matters. Death alone made it possible for the younger brother to test his wings. Even if he couldn't admit it, in early 1944, Singer symbolically killed his father—his second father, the one who had initiated him into the secular world, the world of art and women. Now, like it or not, no other Singer towered above him as a writer— neither Israel Joshua nor Pinchos Menahem, whose writing gifts he had always acknowledged. He was no longer subject to any moral or aesthetic judgment. Not only were the paths of creation now open to him, but it was his obligation, as the last surviving Singer brother, to take over from Joshua and follow in his footsteps.

Singer's fortieth year thus marked the end of a cycle. After wandering for eight and a half years in a psychological no-man's-land, Singer began his second life—his American life, as a citizen and husband—and his real career as a writer. The previous year, the New York publisher Farlag Matones had published *Satan in Goray* in Yiddish, along with some short stories ("The Destruction of Kreshev," "From the Diary of One Not Born," "Zeidlus the Pope," and "Two Corpses Go Dancing").[7] But how pleased could a forty-year-old writer be with only a reissued novel and a handful of short stories to his name? Singer had already lived almost half his life; he had no more time to lose. At forty, he threw himself into fiction again. He was a late bloomer, but from then on he never stopped writing until the very last years of his life.

ASA HESHEL, OR THE BIRTH OF A FAVORITE PROTAGONIST

Among his papers Singer had the draft of an abandoned novel, the story of a Jewish family living in Warsaw between 1912 and 1939. He reshaped the plot, recast the chapters, and went to the library, where he combed through the Polish newspapers of the prewar period, culling anecdotes, news items, and even weather reports. He dug deep into his own memory so the narrative would be not only a historical reconstruction, but also a poignant novel about the slow decline of a formerly wealthy dynasty. The family's quarrels, love stories, and passions are set against the background of the First World War, the Russian Revolution, the Pilsudski regime, and the Nazi invasion. The novel became *The Family Moskat* (*Die Familie Mushkat*). It contains some of Singer's favorite themes: doomed love, the helplessness of the Jewish people, the world wrestling with its blindness. The novel is dedicated to Joshua, a "spiritual father," a "model of high morality and literary honesty," a "modern man" who "had all the great qualities of our pious ancestors." Another telltale sign of Joshua's influence is the fact that Isaac adopted the genre of the family chronicle, the genre of his brother's last book, *The Family Carnovsky* (1943), which describes the assimilation of three generations of German Jews. He remained faithful to the family chronicle in *The Manor* and *The Estate*.

In this narrative panorama, teeming with protagonists, the main figure is Asa Heshel, the fundamentally indecisive character who dreams his life away, much to the misfortune of the three women who cross his path. This tormented individual, caught between his weaknesses and evasiveness, very much resembles Singer himself, apart from a few variations. In this first long novel, Isaac gives us a portrait of the artist as a young man. We find the Krochmalna Street boy who never stops asking questions: How high is the sky? How deep the Earth? What lies at the other side of the world? We recognize this child, a voracious reader whose intelligence drives his entourage to despair—"His grandmother would put her hands to her ears. 'He drives me crazy,' she wailed. 'He's a dybbuk, not a child!' "[8] We meet Todros, renamed Jakuthiel, the Bilgoraj watchmaker and humanist with whom Isaac discussed philosophy. We watch the development of a multifaceted mind, assailed by doubts, fantasies, and desires. Like Singer, Asa, with the frail silhouette of a worried intellectual, moves on the sidelines: always slightly in the background, no matter where he is; simultaneously proud and vulnerable; skeptical yet obsessed with his relationship with God; too lucid to accept the dogma of the law, yet plagued by endless metaphysical doubt.

Here we find Isaac in a nutshell. Before meeting Alma, Singer lost no time in duplicating his many parallel lives in New York. As in Warsaw, he juggled furnished rooms. He had as many as three at the same time—two in Brooklyn and one in Manhattan, on Seventieth Street; he received a different girlfriend in each. In *The Family Moskat*, the "female triangle" first appears in his work. Asa is at the center, torn between three women, none of whom fully satisfies him. Like Singer, he surrenders passively to the chaotic undercurrent of a reality over which he has no control. He submits to marriage with one woman, lets another take him to Switzerland, and is seduced by a third, a Communist reminiscent of Runya. However, he is neither a cynic nor a weakling, but a complex being, too intelligent not to see that truth is disseminated everywhere, scattered among thousands of contradictory polarities. Between fidelity and infidelity, faith and incredulity, tradition and modernity, no single solution is valid on its own. Hence Asa is forced into a zigzagging pattern of behavior, as was Singer throughout his life, attracted by one thing, then drawn like a magnet by another, forever driven by an intense need for the absolute.

In that respect, *The Family Moskat* is a seminal work. Part fiction, part self-portrait, in it Singer creates the prototype of his favorite protagonist, the first in a long line of men partly modeled on himself.

Herman Broder in *Enemies*, Yasha in *The Magician of Lublin*, Grein in *Shadows on the Hudson*: these are all variations on the same recurrent and haunting individual, whom it is hard not to see as an avatar of Isaac himself. "None is really me, but there's a bit of me in all of them," Singer said in corroboration. "I would say I am half Yasha, half Herman . . . I would say that Herman is what I really was and Yasha is maybe what I wanted to be."[9]

In November 1945, the first installment of *The Family Moskat* appeared in the *Jewish Daily Forward*. Serialization continued until May 1948. Two years later, the novel was published in book form in Yiddish by the publisher Morris Sklarsky. That same year, it was translated into English and published by Alfred A. Knopf. The Singer antihero made his debut. In the area of art and literature, this small, unstable, sensitive Jewish intellectual prefigures many others. "Place this protagonist in a New York or Chicago setting, add a comic twist, and the result will be Herzog, Saul Bellow's hero," wrote a reviewer in *Le Monde* when *The Family Moskat* came out in French.[10] Add even more humor—while preserving the serious and ironic undertone—and you are not far from a Woody Allen character.

So, in 1948, Isaac's frame of mind had changed completely. He stopped being the "failure" whom Alma had to take on faith when he assured her he really was a writer—she knew no Yiddish and spoke to Isaac only in English. Singer had found his creative powers again. He adjusted to life in America. He began to love New York, for its vitality and freedom. He sometimes took the el train, from one end of the line to the other, for the sheer pleasure of seeing Manhattan spread out before him. He spent an endless amount of time in cafeterias, where it seemed miraculous that you could eat and sit for the whole day, reading and writing, for just thirty cents. He roamed the streets, daydreamed on the buses and on the Staten Island ferry. He was relieved. He felt free. He was a new man.

AN AILING LANGUAGE

Another great change occurred in Isaac's life. English was no longer an obstacle for him. When he first arrived in the United States, he knew how to say only "Take a chair." After a year of English classes, he could make himself understood and could even—as one might expect—flirt with his teachers. Instead of his usual indecisiveness and vacillation, he showed a staunch determination. He bought index cards on which he noted new words every day, as if to be "author of a dictionary," he said. He also tried to read the Bible in English. Ten years later, though he still had a strong Yiddish accent, pronouncing *w*'s like *v*'s ("I vill tell you, my dahlink"), he was completely fluent and had an extensive vocabulary. He said he felt he had learned the language "thoroughly." "My desire to learn English was very strong. I knew that if I didn't learn this language I would be lost forever. Immigrants seldom really learn English thoroughly, except such a master of language as Nabokov. Of course, I never intended to write in English. I knew that I would write in Yiddish all my life."[11]

This was true. Singer wrote in Yiddish to the end of his life, on the old typewriter Joshua had given him when he first arrived in America. He made this decisive choice with *The Family Moskat*; his work would be crafted in a marginal language, and one that was dying, to boot. Quite a paradox for a writer who aspired to universal recognition! But there were many reasons for this decision. In a sense, he was simply following a natural inclination. Yiddish was spoken in his mother's kitchen; it was the language of his childhood, the one in which he expressed himself in the *Forward*. It was also the language of his protagonists. Even when he set his fiction in America, his heroes were Yiddish-speaking Jews; why would he express himself in a language different from theirs? If he wanted his work to sound authentic, he had no choice. "I felt that Yiddish and the Jewish people and their language were important for me and that if I wanted to be a real writer I would have to write about them and not about the American Gentiles of whom I knew nothing. I had to remember my youth and to stay with my language and with the people I knew best. An assimilated writer never does this. He tries always to go into a group where he does not completely belong."[12]

Yiddish is an unusually rich language. According to linguists, it first appeared in the Rhineland in the ninth century. It is similar to medieval German, the "high middle German" spoken between 1100 and 1500. But it also includes elements from Hebrew, Aramaic, and the Romance and Slavic languages. Over the centuries, Yiddish adopted thousands of words, idioms, and images from these languages. "It results from an alchemy that combined these various origins into something completely original," notes Rachel Ertel. "The Yiddish language is thus a metaphor for Jewish life, and this alchemy created a literature in its own image, that absorbed and changed the world in a specific manner and that is part of European modernity, in the tradition of Schnitzler, Döblin, and Joseph Roth."[13]

It would be difficult for a writer to discard such raw material. Singer has no hesitation about saying that Yiddish is the richest language in the world. Not in scientific and technical vocabulary, of course, but "in creating words which describe character and personality." "It was Freudian before Freud," he says. "It has told many things about our subconscious in its own primitive fashion." He notes, too, that since Yiddish has been used less than other languages, "it still contains quite a number of adjectives and idioms which don't reek of banality."[14] Last, but certainly not least, one of the charms of Yiddish is its humor. For example:

> Take such words as: "A poor man." How many expressions are there in English for poor? You can say: "a poor man, a pauper, a beggar, a mendicant, a panhandler," and this exhausts all that can be said about it. But in Yiddish you can say: "A poor schlemiel, a begging shlimazl, a pauper with dimples, a schnorrer multiplied by eight, a schlepper by the grace of God, an alms collector with a mission, a delegate from the Holy Land, a messenger from a Yeshiva, a miracle worker without a following, a Rabbi without a congregation, a poorhouse resident, a hungerman, a flying wanderer, a warden for his own needs, a squire with a hole, a barefoot count, an owner of a cabbage head, a bag carrier, a house-to-house visitor, dressed in seven coats of poverty, a crumb-catcher, a bone-picker, a plate licker, a daily observer of the Yom Kippur fast," and more.[15]

Yiddish was full of energy and life, a language that was an integral part of his literary ambitions. Nevertheless, Singer was well aware that his choice of Yiddish was by no means the simplest. He knew he had decided to write in an ailing, indeed a dying, language—"the language of no one," to use the poet Paul Celan's grim expression, borrowed by Rachel Ertel. Ten years earlier, when Singer first arrived in New York, Yiddish had been thriving. (True, it always had a paradoxical status. Though it was the principal spoken language of the Jews, it was viewed with contempt, as inferior. Hebrew was the language with prestige; Yiddish was often defined as a dialect.) In those days, there were eleven million Yiddish speakers in the world; after the Shoah, only five to six million remained. Another fundamental change occurred. Before the war, there was a readership for Yiddish writers both in America and in Europe. Europe was the wider audience for what was being created in the United States. "With the disappearance of European Jewry and its language, the simple problem of readership arises," remarks Rachel Ertel. "How is one to write, and for whom, in a language that has almost no audience?"[16]

Singer was perfectly aware that he ran the risk of preaching into the void. Raised in an assimilated family, Alma never concealed her doubts from him: What was the point of being a Yiddish writer after the Second World War? What kind of career could he hope for? Wasn't it an absurd and limiting choice? Singer pondered these questions but came to no conclusion. True, he could have decided to write only for the surviving Yiddish speakers. But this milieu wasn't particularly fond of him. As in Warsaw, the critics complained that he strayed too far from the classical Yiddish tradition, neglected social problems, and was overly preoccupied with sexual issues. That was the last straw!

For all these reasons, he might well have been tempted to change languages. After all, Conrad, Nabokov, and others had done it before him. Even Joshua had considered switching to German or English at one time in his career. Isaac had a gift for languages. He was proficient, in varying degrees, in five: Yiddish, Polish, German, English, and Hebrew. In his youth he had tried to write in Hebrew, showing that the choice of language had already been on his mind. His main desire was to make a name for himself. He therefore had to find a way of giving himself universal stature as a writer. He couldn't be the spokesman for only one inward-looking ethnic group.

What makes Isaac genuine was that he didn't switch languages.

He wasn't, deep down, the opportunist he was later so often accused of being. He never abandoned the language of his fathers, this magnificent, scorned language that conveyed an array of memories, traditions, legends, and the very roots of a people constantly displaced by history. His language was his territory and he knew it. In fact, it is significant that he saw this choice as determined by desire, not ability. Write in English? He doesn't say he can't; it's just that he never intended to. He "knew"—with deep certainty—that he would write in Yiddish all his life.

After the Holocaust, no further doubt was possible. Isaac said so explicitly: the work he wanted to fashion would also be a surviving testimony to a murdered people, a vanished culture, and a dying language. This preoccupation is already present in *The Family Moskat*. Singer wanted to write about the Jewish Warsaw that no one would ever know again. Asking to be forgiven for the comparison, he said in response to Richard Burgin, "Just like Homer . . . felt about Troy, I felt about Warsaw in my own small way."[17]

His notion of responsibility went hand in hand with his view of literature. That was a fortunate coincidence. Singer was convinced that "literature is completely connected with one's origin, with one's roots." He reiterated this constantly: Writers are "all rooted in their people." The masters he admired, "Tolstoy, Dostoyevsky, and Gogol were as Russian, as Ukrainian as they could be."[18] He, Isaac, wanted to be as Polish Jewish as he could be, even in America. He wanted to write stories that only he could have written. He didn't believe in the cosmopolitan novel, portraying protagonists without roots. He was convinced that the writer, more than any other kind of artist, belongs to his culture and language. This was yet another of Isaac's deep paradoxes: he never ceased fusing fanatical individualism with a strong attachment to his origins. Once again, he had found a marvelous way of being both inward- and outward-looking at the same time.

As Hannah Arendt notes, one's native language is all that remains. Up to this point, Singer's life had been a series of ruptures—breaks with religious orthodoxy, with his native Poland, with the mother of his child, with his son, with his brother. The only thing to which he chose to remain faithful was his language. Much as if, after having abandoned everything (or betrayed everything?), he wanted to remain attached to the last thread that still tied him to the world of yesterday. Was it a fear of assimilation? Guilt? Perhaps. But Singer also ardently believed that disowning one's language was, for him, the ultimate betrayal. Abandoning it would be like disowning his very substance.

In a television interview, Singer used a single word to aptly capture his allegiance to his native tongue: he said he was *devoted* to Yiddish. He had no reason to stop writing in Yiddish just because Hitler had killed so many of its speakers. It would be like completing Hitler's job. Perhaps, very soon, only a handful of Yiddish writers would remain, but that made no difference. He would continue to write in Yiddish even if he were the last man to do so.

Responsibility, moral imperative—when it came to language, Isaac showed himself to be utterly faithful. But it was a momentous decision, quite a gamble, to set out writing an entire body of work about a vanished world in a dying language. For the reader in Kentucky or Arkansas, he might as well have been describing daily life in Machu Picchu in the language of the Incas. Starting with *The Family Moskat*, Singer knew that he would have to show boundless ingenuity and talent to win the hearts of non-Jewish readers and truly conquer America.

SEVEN

The Conquest of America

New York, spring 2002. On the corner of Broadway and Eighty-sixth Street, a white-haired man searches through a trash can. A heavyset Rollerblader with earphones whizzes by drinking a cup of coffee. No one seems to pay the slightest attention to the blue sign next to the traffic light: WEST 86TH STREET: ISAAC BASHEVIS SINGER BOULEVARD. Nearby is the Belnord apartment house, a large, elegant building of stone and gray brick, with two entrances leading to a large oval courtyard. The inner courtyard instantly appealed to Isaac. With its garden surrounded by railings and its blooming rhododendrons, it is a protected space, invisible from the street. It reminded him of the courtyard of his childhood, on Krochmalna Street. This was where he lived almost until his death.

From one courtyard to another: Eighty-sixth Street marked a new stage in Isaac's life. He had been living on the Upper West Side for a long time. He had spent many years on 101st Street, near Central Park West, and then on Seventy-second Street, not far from Columbus Avenue. But in the 1960s, something changed. The image Isaac projected to the neighborhood residents was of a cheerful man who went out every day in a suit and hat to feed the pigeons. He became a familiar figure, radiating Old World elegance. People recognized him in cafeterias, or in the Steinberg Dairy Restaurant, one of his favorite Broadway eateries, and they often requested his autograph. Isaac had become a well-known writer, part of the American literary landscape.

What had happened over the course of a dozen years? How had the shy, unhappy Yiddish author turned into a writer with a devastating sense of humor, able to win over audiences with just a few phrases? How had Yitskhok Bashevis become I. B. Singer, the "magician of West 86th Street"?[1]

SAUL BELLOW, THE INTERMEDIARY

The metamorphosis began in 1953. That year, two literary critics, Eliezer Greenberg and Irving Howe, were preparing an anthology of Yiddish short stories to be published in English translation. Greenberg showed Howe the Yiddish text of "Gimpel the Fool" ("Gimpel tam"), exclaiming, "Singer has to be heard to be believed." Howe praised its "verbal and rhythmic brilliance" and saw it was "the work of a master."[2] They had to find a translator. Howe and Greenberg thought of Saul Bellow: same roots, same native language. But Bellow turned them down: he was finishing *The Adventures of Augie March*; between the novel and his courses at Princeton, he had no free time. Greenberg wouldn't take no for an answer. He suggested meeting Bellow and reading him the short story aloud; that way Bellow could sit at the typewriter and translate directly from dictation. Bellow agreed. The result was a powerful, colorful, fluid translation. Even today, it remains one of the most beautiful English translations ever made of a Singer short story.

"Gimpel the Fool" was to be included in *A Treasury of Yiddish Stories*, Howe and Greenberg's anthology, published by Viking Press in 1954. But in the meantime, the authors decided to submit it to *Partisan Review*. It was published in the May 1953 issue—a surprising short story, well served in its translation by a prominent writer; the readers of the *Partisan Review* were immediately captivated. A year later, the journal published another Singer short story, "From the Diary of One Not Yet Born." From then on, things gradually gathered momentum. That same year, *Midstream* published "The Wife Killer"; in 1957, *New World Writing* put out "The Mirror," while *Commentary* published "The Gentleman from Cracow" and "Fire." Singer's fame in the English-speaking world grew with each published story. Soon *Made-*

moiselle, *Esquire*, *Harper's*, *The Saturday Evening Post*, *Playboy*, and *The Reporter* were added to the list. Isaac was making a name for himself.

Unquestionably, Singer owed this big break to Bellow. With Bellow as intermediary, Singer reached the larger, non-Yiddish-speaking public; Bellow's name and prestige launched him into the American literary world. This wasn't the first time Singer had been translated into English. *The Family Moskat* had been published by Knopf in 1950 with no comparable impact. This time, one translation led to another. Thanks to Bellow, Singer had bridged the gap between Yiddish and English, between the Old World and the New.

But Singer never showed Bellow the slightest gratitude. After his breakthrough, Singer even saw to it that Bellow never translated any of his other stories. He made a point of seeing him as infrequently as possible. This is reminiscent of the cool and aloof attitude with which Isaac had often treated his brother. He knew he owed his life to Joshua but preferred to keep him at a distance; he owed Bellow the start of his career in English but carefully kept him from any further involvement.

Was this ingratitude on Singer's part, or the desire not to be beholden to anyone? Whatever the case, Bellow never forgave him. "Bellow was very angry at Singer," explains Robert Giroux, Isaac's editor at Farrar, Straus and Giroux for thirty-five years. "Needless to say, Bellow didn't consider himself 'a translator' and felt Singer owed him gratitude. He expected Isaac to thank him, but Isaac never did— possibly out of pride. Or because he had been so humiliated in his youth, living in the shadow of his brother, whom everyone praised. Yes, Isaac was cold and self-controlled. He wasn't a toady at all."[3]

Years later, Bellow met Singer at a cocktail party and asked him why he had never wanted him to translate any of his other short stories. Isaac's reply was disarming: if the translations had been too good, the public would have confused translator and author. "They'll say it's you, not me." His casual dismissal infuriated Bellow. He settled his score with Singer in a number of interviews. Singer, he said, without mincing words, was never the innocent storyteller he pretended to be. "He was sophisticated. He was an opportunist. He was a careerist."[4]

Opportunist: this label stuck to him for years to come, at least in Yiddish-speaking circles. The goyim applauded him while the Jews gave him the cold shoulder. That was the crowning irony. What grudge did they bear him? First of all, they resented the fact that he was translated. Most Yiddish writers of the period were not, and they were bitter about it. But jealousy wasn't the only factor. They also resented him for orchestrating the transposition of his work into English in a way that maximized its chances of being liked by a wide American public.

FROM YIDDISH TO ENGLISH: SINGER'S SYSTEM

In fact, after 1954, Singer adopted a hands-on approach to the translation of his books into English. Officially, he wanted to improve on the original Yiddish. Every week, he delivered two chapters of his novel-in-progress to the *Forward*. Each serialized installment had to be two thousand words. There were times when his weekly text fell short and he had to pad it with anecdotes or descriptions. Translation was the perfect opportunity for getting rid of the filler, and Isaac took full advantage of it. He trimmed, made cuts, tightened his narratives until they were worthy of publication in book form.

But his work extended far beyond that. Singer's Yiddish texts are learned and erudite, peppered with quotes from the Hebrew and Aramaic. "It's as if a present-day French author were to lard his pages with Latin and Greek," explains Delphine Bechtel, assistant professor of German and Yiddish studies at the Sorbonne. "Even specialists occasionally have to resort to an Aramaic dictionary."[5] Isaac constantly refers to his biblical and Talmudic methods of argument, to a typically Jewish kind of casuistry. So much so that his work in Yiddish is really directed at only a small circle of initiates, whose intellectual upbringing is similar to his own.

Isaac was well aware that his Yiddish oeuvre was too coded to transpose into English dialect. Could an American reader in Minnesota glean anything from his biblical Hebrew? Or from his veiled references to the Ashkenazi imaginative tradition? Translation from the Yiddish, in the normal sense, would have required dozens of footnotes, which was unthinkable. His Yiddish writings had to be thoroughly reworked, adapted, reconceived. This was something only he himself could do.

Isaac cut and eliminated entire sections of the Yiddish text. "He developed a philosophy of the wastebasket as the writer's most essential tool, identical to God's in the creation process," notes Henri Lewi.

He pared his text to the bone, keeping only the indispensable elements of the setting and the details essential to the story line. The rest—the Hebrew, the Aramaic, the inbred allusions, the anti-Christian quips—all these things were written off as losses.

Most important is the deletion of the original Hebrew, the Christianization of the text. David Roskies[6] has shown that *a shnur patsherkes*, meaning literally (and not without mockery) "Pater cord," becomes "rosary"; the word *galekh*, a rude term for a Christian priest ("the closely cropped one"), is changed to "sacristan"; "house of impurity" expresses an external, hostile point of view; "rosary" and "sacristan" are Christian words that Polish Jewish readers may not have understood.[7]

Singer thus invented a kind of "literary correctness" before the fact. He made his texts not only more readable but also more acceptable to WASP readers. He even changed the protagonists and altered the endings and entire passages of his stories!

Examples abound. Take the short story "The Mirror," in which a demon installed inside a mirror goes about debauching a pretty young woman named Zirel. As a personal experiment, the Yiddish specialist Batia Baum translated this story from Yiddish into French. A passage from her French translation, here translated into English, allows us to compare the Yiddish and English versions of the same story. The ending of "The Mirror," from Singer's original Yiddish, is as follows:

Is there a God? Is He all merciful? Did He create the world? Did He give the world the Torah? Will the Messiah come? Will the prophet Elijah blow the ram's horn on the Mount of Olives and announce the resurrection of the dead? Does sainthood duel against impurity? Will God combat Satan? Or is the demon justified in his pretensions, and is he the prince of princes? What does a minor devil know about who runs the world? He who wants to know is whipped around. Deep down in my heart, under cover, I'm an atheist. There is nothing except atoms. All the worlds are vile fungi. An inkwell fell upside down off its base, spilling ink; the ink was carried away by the wind, scattered, smeared up and down, across and in depth, and this resulted in a letter, an endless incoherent piece of writing, a roll that is un-rolled ad infinitum, a story without end, an *aleph* that never reaches the *tov*. Judge only by what your eyes see. Everything was and remains mere confusion, emptiness, and chaos.

But then on second thought, who knows? Perhaps, never-theless? What if the demons were to lose their power? Perhaps the great Innocent one will achieve his ends at the end of time? In the meanwhile, we're the bosses. In the meanwhile, the world is a world with no judge or justice. Even the finest flower is full of bran. And me, a little nothing imp, tossed about from everywhere, I am nestling once again inside a mirror, lying in wait for a fresh young woman, a new victim for the devil. As Joseph della Reina says, you don't throw away the im-pure before finding the pure. God is an enigma, and doubt within doubt. The Other Side, the devil, is vile but concrete. Between the certain and the maybe, the certain is better. I stud-ied at heder and know the Talmud.[8]

In the English version, all these metaphysical questions—the same ones that tormented the little boy on Krochmalna Street—have com-pletely vanished. Singer concludes his short story as follows:

Is there a God? Is He all merciful? Will Zirel ever find salva-tion? Or is creation a snake primeval crawling with evil? How can I tell? I'm still only a minor devil. Imps seldom get pro-moted. Meanwhile generations come and go, Zirel follows Zirel, in a myriad of reflections—a myriad of mirrors.[9]

What a difference!

Sometimes we come upon the opposite. The Yiddish doesn't exist and the English has been created ex nihilo. For example, the novel *Shosha* is a reworking of the autobiographical novel *Neshome ekspedit-*

sies (Expeditions of the Soul), which was serialized in the *Forward* but never published as a book. The first chapter of *Shosha* doesn't exist in the serialized Yiddish version; the beginning is completely different. Similarly, the English chapters 12 and 14 have no corresponding Yiddish text. They were added, probably directly in English, since, to this day, researchers have found no Yiddish versions of them.[10]

We can see how unsuitable the term "translation" is to these transpositions from one language to another. Singer created a second corpus alongside his Yiddish one; the two are neither completely identical nor completely different. Two different creations, conceived in two distinct languages, two visions of the world intended for two separate readerships. Where is the "real Singer" in all this? He is perpetually "between" the two: between Yiddish and English, Warsaw and New York, father and son, the living and the dead, between Yitskhok and Isaac, between himself and his double.

Singer has no precedent in the history of literature. What other great writer can claim the paternity of two differently centered bodies of work? We might think of Kafka, his writings in German and their translation into other languages; or of Nabokov, who switched from Russian to English at age forty-two. But there is no other example exactly like Singer's. The only remotely comparable case is that of Kundera, who at one point decided personally to review all the French translations of his books in order to give them the same authenticity as the original Czech.[11] The fact is, Singer regarded his works in English as forming an original body of work, on a par with his Yiddish oeuvre. A "second original" is what he insistently called it. Singer set up no hierarchical difference between his works in Yiddish and his works in English; true, they were different, but he regarded them as having the *same artistic importance*. So much so that it was from the English, and not the Yiddish, that he wanted his works translated into all other languages.

TWO LANGUAGES, TWO BODIES OF WORK

This is what many Yiddish scholars find hard to accept. They see it as incomprehensibly odd, a repudiation of Yiddish, an ambivalence toward his native language that they find inexplicable. They are frustrated at not being allowed to publish translations from the Yiddish because Singer himself opposed it.

"I don't know if the meaning of this has been properly gauged," Henri Lewi notes. "A writer who gives up the text he has produced in his own language, a very strong, subtle, linguistically rich text; who forbids using it, consigns it to the dust, dooms it to oblivion, and apparently doesn't even consider having it published for future readers who might appreciate it; and treats it like a first draft that should be forgotten, lost, and thrown in the wastebasket."[12]

A first draft! Yet Yiddish scholars stress the exceptional quality of the work in Yiddish. They regard the works in English as "popularized" and of lesser merit. This is why many of them plead for a reading of Singer in his native language.[13]

"For me, the second body of work is an inferior body of work," explains Lewi, one of the rare people to have made a comparative study of the two. "The English translation is good. But with the Hebrew eliminated, the rhythm of the original language is lost. In the Yiddish versions, the Hebrew is a way of giving emphasis to the text. It conveys the great concepts of the Ashkenazi Jews' world vision. It is the writer's wellspring, the world of his childhood, his father, the liturgy."[14]

If only outsiders had disfigured Isaac's work in English! If only he could have been seen as a powerless victim! Then these people could have made a big fuss and quickly restored the text to its original "true" version. But the fact is, it was Isaac himself who was responsible for the transformation; it was he who dared assert that neither version was more authentic than the other and who refused to let the Yiddish text be the exclusive original; this is what many people found so disconcerting. It led to countless accusations of treason and opportunism, and to the persistence with which, even today, his detractors seek explanations for the "inexplicable."

A first hypothesis: Singer knew how to sell himself. "His American versions are more commercial than the Yiddish versions," says Delphine Bechtel. "He knows he is addressing a puritanical public. He preserves a bit of sex, but not too much. He mixes together the ingredients of the timeless Jewish novel—the rabbi, the perverse woman, the seduced student. Most of the holidays are there. And the Jewish picturesque . . . it has to be appealing."[15]

A second hypothesis: Singer was fully aware that the English translations had less value than the Yiddish texts, but he didn't want to antagonize his American publisher. "In the beginning," claims Khoné Shmeruk of the Hebrew University in Jerusalem, "Singer said quite clearly that no translation would be able to capture everything contained in the Yiddish original. Later he changed his mind. I don't think it is because his translations had improved, but because, I'm afraid, of pressure from the publisher and self-interest."[16]

Treason or extreme faithfulness? The debate continues. We need only listen to a confrontation between Henri Lewi and Seth Wolitz, professor of literature at the University of Texas at Austin, to understand how irreconcilable these two points of view are: "With 'Gimpel the Fool,' Singer understood that he had captured a public whose existence he hadn't imagined," asserts Wolitz. "He gauged the immense nostalgia of all the third- and fourth-generation American Jews, all the assimilated Jews, who were eager to know more about their roots and Eastern Europe. He wanted to be liked by these readers, whom he believed to be his sole future. Thus he accepted the compromises he needed to make."

Impossible, retorts Lewi. "Singer was an extremely scrupulous writer. Every little comma was important. Writing, regardless of the language, is not an innocent game. Singer . . . searched for the right word in English as meticulously as he had searched for it in Yiddish. In the end he was satisfied with the English text, a text he saw as genuinely English . . . the original raised to the universal, to the extent that English, today, represents the universal."[17]

Going back to the primary sources sheds light on this debate. Examination of the manuscripts shows that Henri Lewi is right: Singer was meticulous in his choice of words. The enormous typed manuscript of *The Manor* in English—979 pages on India paper, available at Columbia University in New York—is full of green, red, and blue pencil marks. There is a second version in which these changes are incorporated and many others added. Isaac hesitated with the very first sentence. Should there be one verb or two? He adds a verb, crosses it out, puts it back: a process of trial and error showing an almost obsessive concern with rhythm, musicality, equilibrium. The Yiddish typescript of *The Slave* is also kept at Columbia; it seems to have been reread just as carefully as the proofs in English, where Isaac even replaced contemporary terms with words in Old English. The manuscripts of *Short Friday and Other Stories* give us the best idea of how much time Singer devoted right up to publication. The Yiddish text of each short story was revised when it was first translated into English for various periodicals (*Commentary, Mademoiselle, Midstream, Prism*). Then Singer reworked the printed texts for the book versions. After that, he corrected the anthology proofs. In other words, there were no fewer than four drafts between the *Forward* version and the printed book, three of which were in English.

This kind of work isn't typical of an opportunist. On the contrary, it typifies a stylist, a perfectionist, someone fanatical about his craft. How can we explain what happened in the 1950s? Why did Isaac begin to construct two bodies of work, an unprecedented enterprise about which he kept strangely silent? Opportunism? Sheer ambition? There is a third explanation, probably the most plausible: faithfulness.

A FORM OF ULTIMATE FIDELITY

In 1953, when Singer realized that his work had a universality capable of moving a wide audience, the question of translation became absolutely vital to him.

Having been a translator himself (of Knut Hamsun and Thomas Mann, among others), he was acutely aware of the difficulties of the profession. "A translation, like a woman, can be true and faithful and still miserable," he often said in jest.[18] In fact, he had learned a lesson several years earlier with the translation from Yiddish into German of *The Family Moskat*, one he considered disastrous. Above all, Isaac knew that unfortunately, with time, there would be fewer and fewer Yiddish translators. That was why he decided to rewrite his work in English himself: to salvage the best part of it, to establish a universal referent that nothing could bury, neither history nor time.

This did not prevent him from continuing to write and publish books in Yiddish—in the *Forward*, with Morris Sklarsky or Farlag Matones—though he could have stopped at any time. He created another body of work, inextricably embedded in the language and, in a certain sense, untranslatable. This is why he did not encourage any attempts. A veil, or curtain, protects the works in Yiddish from the general public. Like an unapproachable woman, the Yiddish works are jealously guarded and hidden in the background—which doesn't mean they are superior to the English works in literary value, merely different.

Why were they kept at a distance? We may well wonder whether Singer's secret desire was to hide his Yiddish oeuvre in order to better preserve it, like a treasure he wanted to keep for the "happy few." This would be a rather protectionist approach, but it should not be seen as a betrayal; rather, it is his proud and original way of respecting the intimate secrets of languages, demonstrating an extreme fidelity to his original culture.

AN INDUSTRIAL METHODOLOGY

There are indeed two bodies of work: one for Yiddish speakers and the other for everyone else (including the assimilated Jews, for whom Singer did not always have the greatest respect). At this stage in his career, Singer became both writer and strategist, gambling openly on English as a passport to posterity but never forsaking the language of his own people. It's as though he were writing in yesterday's language with his left hand and in tomorrow's language with his right. We need hardly point out his enormous capacity for work. Imagine Balzac simultaneously constructing a second body of work! Isaac set up an almost industrial methodology in the fifties, a discipline he adhered to until the end of his life.

What a difference between the misfit living in furnished rooms and the writer of West Eighty-sixth Street! Isaac hardly had time to read and went out very rarely. His entire life revolved around his work. He would wake up every morning at seven o'clock and spend two hours thinking about the story he was working on. Lying in bed, he would fill up his notebooks—always the same kind—which he brought with him when he traveled: "I have to write in notebooks with lined paper, but without the vertical red-line margin you find in so many notebooks, because I write from right to left and the margin only confuses me. They don't seem to make these anymore [indicating notebooks he has brought with him to Europe], but I've hoarded a supply and I know that the Kresge chain somehow still carries them. When I'm on a lecture tour I always ask my hosts to take me to Kresge."[19]

"By the time those two hours of concentration were over, the story was thoroughly structured and woven, with all its details," reports Israel Zamir. "At nine o'clock he put his thin feet on the scale next to his bed and examined the needle for a long time to make sure he hadn't put on any weight."[20] It was out of the question for him to grow soft and fat, or "to carry a whole grocery store around on [his] body." In Warsaw and New York, he had suffered from enough hunger and poverty to stick to the principle that the body "must take only" what it needs.[21] After checking that he hadn't gained any weight, Isaac hurried to the bathroom and spent about half an hour in his bath, still pondering his plot. Then he slipped on his gray robe, always the same one, and ate breakfast quickly so he could get his thoughts down on paper.

Serialization in the *Forward* imposed great discipline on him as well. When he began a novel, he had to finish it. His readers were waiting for the next installment. He had to deliver "copy" every week. But this constraint suited him. "An artist, like a horse, needs a whip," Isaac said. He grew so accustomed to this pace that it became "second nature." Toward the end of his life, he congratulated himself on never having missed a deadline. "I haven't missed a week in all these years, except that I get four weeks' vacation. But then I work harder than ever in preparing copy for after the vacation."[22]

This was true. From the early seventies to the mid-eighties, Isaac and Alma spent one summer month per year in Wengen, Switzerland, in the company of Marie-Pierre Bay and her family and other foreign publishers, including his German publisher, Christoph Schlotterer, and his Swedish publisher, Dorotea Bromberg. He maintained the same self-imposed discipline on vacation.

Marie-Pierre Bay saw this discipline as the rules of orthodoxy, which had so dominated his childhood, reasserting themselves, transposed onto the secular world:

> The Jewish, unlike the Catholic religion, does not just consist in going to mass, praying, receiving the sacraments . . . It takes over every aspect of everyday life. If you are a practicing Jew, there is something to do or not do every hour of the day. Isaac's entire youth was marked by this, since his father was ultra-Orthodox. He never escaped from these rhythms and rules. They left their mark on him . . .
>
> When we came to see him in Wengen, he never failed to explain, "We can't see each other in the morning, because I work. Nor in the afternoon because I work." So we agreed to take a walk at lunchtime. But that was also strictly regulated. He came out of his room at noon, with Alma. And we'd set off, because walking and exercise were necessary. He loved walking. He was so fast I sometimes had trouble keeping up with him. We would walk from this hour to that hour, period, and that was it. When we returned, he would go back to work until seven o'clock. Because dinner was at seven o'clock, not seven-ten or five past seven!
>
> After dinner, we would take another walk, which was more relaxed. Then we would chat. Usually we re-created the Warsaw Yiddish Writers' Club. It was very entertaining, but at ten o'clock it was over. He went to bed so he would be in shape for the next morning . . . I think these were old habits deeply ingrained from childhood. He had witnessed his father and mother's extreme rigidity about schedules, rules, prayers. He wasn't religious—his way of life was completely secular—but he was still imbued with a self-imposed, ironclad discipline all the time.[23]

A HAREM OF TRANSLATORS

In New York, Alma was an essential part of this organized life. Quite simply, it was she who supported the couple. Born into a wealthy family, Alma had not really worked before her marriage to Isaac. But up until the fifties, Isaac earned very little. Though *The Family Moskat* sold thirty-five thousand copies in English, his royalties were far from adequate—two thousand dollars, according to Singer, who complained bitterly about it. Alma was the family breadwinner; she began by working in a framer's shop, coming home every evening with her fingers covered with glue and irritated by solvents. Then she worked as a saleswoman at Macy's and, finally, at Lord & Taylor, where she quickly rose up the ranks. She woke every morning at dawn to take the subway. She took charge of everything, relieving her "great man" of all practical tasks. Isaac was incapable of facing life without a helping hand. "He's a genuine writer," she said, "who can't fix himself a meal or wash dishes or do the shopping."[24]

Remember that, after their meeting in the Catskills, Alma had sought out Isaac in New York and had finally found him in the Public Library on Forty-second Street. Madly in love, she had left everything—husband, children, a comfortable life—for a stranger who wrote in a language she didn't understand. She agreed to work so he could write with a clear mind. Without her, without her self-abnegation, Isaac could not have devoted his time to writing, and he knew it. Yet, as might be expected, he was not always grateful to her: "He admired her elegance, respected her rigor, her frankness, her extreme thriftiness," recalls Marie-Pierre Bay. "But this did not prevent him from being nasty to her sometimes. He constantly scolded her over petty things. But Alma considered her devotion normal."[25]

Dorothea Straus, wife of the publisher Roger Straus, goes a step further. "Alma always thought about him before thinking of herself. She was completely devoted to him. Yes, she must have suffered. Her children were very young when she left them, about four and six. Isaac didn't want to see them. She went to visit them by herself from time to time in New Jersey. He never discussed it with her."[26]

This is hardly a surprise. Since Isaac kept his own son at a distance—writing to him, in Israel, only twice a year—he wasn't about to burden himself with someone else's children. What he aspired to was peace and the freedom to devote himself to writing and to women. As far as writing was concerned, he was highly organized.

He wrote in the morning, while Alma worked at Lord & Taylor. He sent his Yiddish copy to the *Forward* every week. As for his English writing, he left Knopf after *The Family Moskat* because he felt they hadn't treated him well. He began publishing with a smaller house, the Noonday Press, which became a subsidiary of Farrar, Straus and Giroux in 1960. Thus, almost by accident, he found his permanent publisher, Farrar, Straus and Giroux. He remained faithful to them to the end of his life.

He was free to write. But what about women? How could Isaac still find time for women, his main source of inspiration and creativity? His stroke of genius consisted in making them a pivotal part of his work strategy. Along with Alma, the *Forward*, and Farrar, Straus and Giroux, there was another sphere of activity in the "Singer system"—his "translators"—without whom he couldn't survive and who gravitated to him constantly.

"In my younger days," Singer wrote, "I used to dream about a harem full of women, lately I'm dreaming about a harem full of translators. If those translators could be women in addition, this would be paradise on earth."[27]

He constructed this paradise in his Upper West Side apartment. While he worked, he was constantly interrupted by the telephone. It was usually his *Forward* readers who wanted to express their admiration. Singer loved this. He always made it a point of honor to be listed in the telephone book, so as not to be deprived of these calls from strangers. When the admirers were female, he eagerly invited them over to discuss his stories. If they happened to be charming, lively, and proficient typists, they stood a chance of becoming one of his "translators" or "secretaries."

This was how the list of his translators started to grow in the mid-fifties. It didn't include only women—Joseph Singer, Isaac's nephew, with whom he subsequently quarreled over money, was certainly one of his most important translators. But women occupied an essential position. One of the first among them was Elaine Gottlieb, the wife of Cecil Hemley, the founder of the Noonday Press. Then there were Mirra Ginsburg, Laurie Colwin, Nancy Gross, Elizabeth Pollet, Elizabeth Shub, Dorothea Straus, and Dvorah Telushkin. They did not all have the same kind of relationship with Singer, but Isaac's way of working was the same with each. He would dictate in English, translating a story published in Yiddish in the *Forward*. Every once in a while, he would stop to find the most appropriate English turn of phrase. This was when the translator made suggestions. In fact, many of these women didn't know Yiddish. They were there to reassure Singer, make him feel confident that his English version had the feel of a genuine American text.

This is corroborated by Dorothea Straus, who started to work with Isaac in the 1960s. At the Lotos Club in New York, forty years later, Roger Straus's wife—an elegant, distinguished-looking woman in a wide-brimmed black hat—puts her role as a translator into perspective:

> Believe me, he didn't need help. He translated perfectly well on his own. He had such a feeling for the language! Could he have written in English? Of course. He had a sense for the tiniest difference between words, the subtlest nuance, and he interrupted himself immediately when it "didn't sound right." Yes, he had what in music we call "perfect pitch." In fact, it's amusing that despite his fine-tuned ear he kept a strong accent. He was always incredibly concentrated when he translated. In fact, he didn't "translate." He "read" the *Forward* aloud directly in English. Very often, I couldn't follow him. He went too fast. It gave me cramps. No, he didn't need a translator at all. The only thing I did, sometimes, was to put the verb in the proper place. Or he would ask, "Dorothea, what is the word for when blood rushes to your cheeks?" I would say, "blush?" And he would sigh, "Oh, what would I do without my translators!"[28]

So all these men and women whose names are listed on most of the English translations were really editors, not translators, says Dorothea Straus. They helped polish the text to a flawless finish. This was important work for Singer, who was publishing more and more short stories in *The New Yorker* and who wanted to submit perfect texts.

When we had finished the work, he would give me seventy-one dollars and three cents. Always the same amount. Don't ask me why. He would say ironically, "It's a pleasure for me to make a check out to a rich woman." Actually, I should have paid him. It was a pleasure to watch him work—a lesson in mental agility! Little by little, the story would take shape. We were in the world of pious rabbis, yeshiva students, miracles, and dybbuks. Isaac was such a born storyteller that, even orally, he kept you in suspense. "That's enough for today," he would say. And I'd have to wait until the next day or the day after to find out how the story ended.[29]

"EVERY WOMAN WHO PASSES BY ON BROADWAY IS A RIDDLE TO ME"

In Isaac's harem, translators were the muses and the Madonnas. They charmed him, inspired him, amused him. "Why should it be essential to love rarely in order to love much?" asks Don Juan in Camus's *The Myth of Sisyphus*. Isaac loved women in all their diversity. He didn't necessarily make them his mistresses. He was sincerely interested in them. He loved their secrets and their life stories—and used them if need be in his books. He wanted to know everything about them, even the most intimate details of their lives. Many describe the intensity with which he stared at his interlocutors, as though he could see through them.

Did he have illusions about their feelings? Not necessarily. But what difference did that make? They were essential to his way of living and to his work. Anything that might disrupt this made Isaac furious.

"One day, during an interview, I said that I didn't know Yiddish and that I couldn't really be introduced as Singer's translator," says Dorothea Straus. "Isaac became terribly angry. 'Stop telling everyone that you're not a translator,' he said to me reproachfully. 'I want women to keep coming to me. If they can't have their name in *The*

New Yorker, they won't come anymore.' Indeed, the translators' names appeared next to his in the pages of the magazine. Whatever the nature of the work they did, Isaac thought it was good for the translator's name to be cited. This symbolic reward, he used to say, was an added reason for all these women to come knocking at his door."[30]

Both in English and in Yiddish, the decade 1953–1963 was a period of intense creativity in Isaac's life. Never before had he been so productive. Never before had he been in such possession of his faculties. He worked obsessively. In Yiddish he published *Shadows on the Hudson* in 1956 and *A Ship to America* in 1957 (which was never translated). In English he published *Satan in Goray* in 1955, *Gimpel the Fool and Other Stories* in 1957, *The Magician of Lublin* in 1960, *The Spinoza of Market Street* in 1961, *The Slave* in 1962, and *Short Friday and Other Stories* in 1964. Creating two bodies of work was in itself a superhuman task. But satisfying both the workaholic and the womanizer was a real tour de force. Alma turned a blind eye. She knew there was nothing she could do: for Isaac, writing and women were inextricably intertwined; his stories took shape thanks to his romantic adventures, real or imagined. Alluding to Herman Broder, the hero of his novel *Enemies*, Singer sighed, " 'I'm Herman, for good and for bad.' He smiled, shrugging his shoulders. 'Does a man have control over his lust? Life is an overflowing sea. Every affair enriched my life and my creativity. No, I'm not sorry. I'm a bachelor . . . in my soul. Even if I married a whole harem of women, I'd still act like a bachelor.' "[31]

The traffic light changes to red on the corner of West Eighty-sixth Street. Different women begin to cross. We might hear Isaac's voice say, "Every woman who passes by on Broadway is a riddle to me."[32] We could see him reincarnated as the demon in *The Mirror*, a pale little man with flaring ears, running after each woman and asking, "Excuse me, ma'am, where are you from? Do you believe in God? In free choice? In reincarnation? What are your relations with your husband?"[33] Then he would whip out his spiral notebook and jot down an anecdote or two, from right to left, in squiggly, tiny Hebrew characters.

If there was one facet of his personality that had not changed, this was it. At sixty, as at seventeen, Singer was the eager servant of his two idols, women and literature. But he was completely changed in every other respect. By the mid-sixties his success in America had further divided him. He was now torn by two languages, two bodies of work, two reading publics. He also wore two masks: the shy Yitskhok Bashevis had spawned a double, I. B. Singer, a celebrated writer people stopped in the street. From then on, these two beings never ceased fighting each other.

EIGHT

Singer Versus Singer

TWO BODIES OF WORK, two identities . . . A far cry from the misanthrope haunted by thoughts of suicide! In the mid-sixties, a new Singer was born. English-speaking Americans called him Isaac. They said he was the most jovial person they knew, the life of the party, whose irresistible, funny stories and gift for paradox made you laugh immediately. For Yiddishists, however, he was still Bashevis, the man with the tortured soul and tortuous mind who had fled Poland. Even today, these two groups appear to be talking about different men. Of course, these divergent views can partly be explained by Singer's growing success. But make no mistake about it: under his serene exterior, Isaac the charmer was struggling against the somber Bashevis. This Polish past soon caught up with him; racked by feelings of guilt and an uneasy conscience, Singer was never at peace with himself.

"BETWEEN A SPRITE AND A BON PAPA"

Yet Singer had every reason to be at peace. His readership was increasing daily. Beginning in the 1960s, universities vied with one another to invite him to give lectures, readings, and courses. Singer adored these occasions. They were welcome pauses in his heavy writing schedule. He traveled all around the country, from Rochester to

Miami, Columbus to California, with set speeches on half a dozen preprepared topics: "Literature and Folklore," "A Personal Concept of Religion," "The Supernatural in Life and Literature," or "My Philosophy as a Jewish Writer." On the latter subject, Isaac always stressed the link he saw between roots and talent. "The richer the soil, the stronger the plant," he used to say. "Literature is completely connected with one's origins, with one's roots."[1] "Dostoyevsky's novel *Crime and Punishment* . . . could not have taken place in China or even anywhere else in Russia."[2] Once again we can see how different Singer's position was from, for example, Bellow's. Bellow repeatedly said to anyone who wished to listen, "I am an American writer who happens to be Jewish." Singer reversed the proposition and said time and time again, "I am a Jewish writer who happens to live in America."

Isaac never forgot to talk about himself—"after all, this is a subject on which I'm an authority," he quipped. He also used these occasions to lay out certain rules for writing and writers. First: A novel has to be based on a story. A plague on modern novelists, he said, who had declared war on the story. The primary aim of literature—and he didn't care if it sounded old-fashioned—was to amaze and captivate. Second rule: The author must have "the conviction, or perhaps the illusion" that he is the only writer who could write this particular story. "No writer in all the world or in any generation could have written *The Death of Ivan Ilyich* but Tolstoy. If I could imagine for a second that a story of mine could be written by another person, this story would be out."[3] Finally, the third rule: Literature has no message (for that "there are Ten Commandments," Singer said).[4] Besides, he added maliciously, "[w]riters can't change the world, we can't even make it worse."[5] In other words, "[a]rt is a force, but without a vector. Like the waves of the sea it flows forward and backward, but the net result is static."[6]

All this may sound dry and theoretical, but for an hour, his audiences were always spellbound. With a broad smile and a twinkle in his eye, Singer looked out at his audience at the end of his lecture and said, in his strongly accented English, "Ladies and gentlemen, ask me any questions you feel like asking. If I know the answer, I vill answer you, and if I don't know the answer, I vill answer you anyhow."[7] The audience laughed in delight. Some of his listeners were renewing their ties with their cultural heritage. Others were discovering a new world of fiction. Many of them felt the urge to follow up with impassioned letters, like the woman in New York State who wrote, "I have never written a 'fan letter' to a writer before, but I felt very strongly that I must give you something in return from the moments of joy and laughter you have given me."[8]

Isaac derived increasing pleasure from these joyous moments as well. Every time he was onstage, it was apparent he was not just a born charmer but also an outstanding entertainer, so much so that one day he expressed the wish to die like Molière, in the middle of a "performance." Moreover, in the sixties, these one-man shows became a significant source of extra income. In 1967, he earned only one hundred and thirty dollars a week at the *Forward*. Yet his records for the year show that he gave more than twenty lectures for the Jewish Center Lecture Bureau: he went to Flint, Michigan; Des Moines, Iowa; Gary, Indiana; Oberlin, Ohio; Birmingham, Alabama; and Winnipeg, Canada. He received five hundred dollars for each lecture; in a single evening, he earned more than three times his weekly salary at the paper. (His lecture fees went up over time: one thousand dollars in Boston in 1972; three thousand dollars in California in 1981; ten thousand dollars at West Point several years later; and so on.)

But even with a growing number of lectures and readings, Singer never relaxed his work schedule. His serialized novels continued to appear in the pages of the *Forward*, while Farrar, Straus and Giroux published *In My Father's Court* in 1966, *The Manor* in 1967, *The Seance and Other Stories* in 1968, *The Estate* and *When Shlemiel Went to Warsaw and Other Stories* in 1969. Magazines were also increasingly eager to publish his short stories. At *The New Yorker*, the editor Rachel McKenzie was extremely enthusiastic about Singer's fiction. She and Isaac admired each other and developed a strong intellectual bond. He began publishing more short stories beginning in 1967. At least eight were printed between April and October 1968, including "A Friend of Kafka," "The Joke," and "The Key." The critics responded favorably. "One of our major creative artists," wrote Curt Leviant in the *Saturday Review*. "Singer's very old-fashionedness becomes a virtue," John Wain proclaimed in *The New York Review of Books*. "Technically, he is a master." Again in the *Saturday Review*, Robert Alter said, "Whatever he does, he remains a gifted storyteller." And Peter Prescott, in *Newsweek*, remarked that his stories celebrated "the dignity, mystery and unexpected joy of living with more art and fervor than any other writer alive."[9]

"Congratulations on all the excitement about your book," Elaine Gottlieb had written him two years earlier, following the publication of *In My Father's Court* in 1966. "Everywhere I look I see a review of it and people keep bringing the reviews to my attention."[10] Indeed, word of mouth was so positive that *In My Father's Court* put a Singer book on the bestseller list for the first time. Sales took off and so did Singer's royalties. Whereas in 1959 his advances from the Noonday Press had been three hundred dollars for *Satan in Goray* and five hundred for *The Magician of Lublin*, a year later Farrar, Straus gave him two thousand dollars for *In My Father's Court*, *The Slave*, and a book of short stories. In 1964, he received twice that amount for only two books. In 1968, Isaac signed a contract for twenty-five thousand dollars for *Enemies*, *The Certificate*, and *Scum*. He couldn't believe it. He, the starving pauper! The Yiddish writer who had struggled for years, living from hand to mouth! To Robert Giroux, who joined him for lunch one day at his apartment on the Upper West Side, he confessed, " 'Robert, one thing I never thought would happen—I've become a rich man.' This," notes the publisher, "was before Hollywood had purchased 'Yentl the Yeshiva Boy' or *Enemies, A Love Story*, before he had won munificent literary prizes, and when his income, though steady, was far from spectacular. Moved by his comment, I could only say, 'Isaac, you ain't seen nothin' yet.' "[11]

AN INTERNATIONAL SUCCESS

Robert Giroux was right. Singer hadn't "seen nothin' yet." Soon he would make a name for himself internationally, starting in Sweden, Germany, and Italy. In France, André Bay brought him to the attention of the public in the sixties. Herbert Lottman, who was the

Street scenes in Jewish Warsaw before the First World War

(Courtesy of Roger Viollet)

Warsaw: the Jewish quarter at the end of the 1930s (Courtesy of Roger Viollet)

Isaac B. Singer as a young
man, circa 1935 (Courtesy of
the Harry Ransom Center, The
University of Texas at Austin)

Singer's son, Israel Zamir, and
Israel's mother, Runya, just
before their departure for the
Soviet Union in 1935 (Courtesy
of D.R.)

New York: a Lower East Side street in a Jewish immigrant neighborhood
(Courtesy of Roger Viollet)

New York, 1930: a protest against the oppression of Jews in Germany (Courtesy of Corbis)

Alma Wasserman—
soon to be Alma
Singer—during the
year she met Isaac
in the Catskills
(Courtesy of D.R.)

Alma and Isaac in Central
Park, 1955 (Courtesy of D.R.)

Singer dictating the translation of a page of the *Forward*,
here with the birds he so loved (Courtesy of Corbis)

Stockholm, 1978: receiving the Nobel Prize (Courtesy of Corbis)

Stockholm, 1978: Singer and his son, the journalist Israel Zamir (Courtesy of Israel Zamir)

Singer feeding pigeons on Broadway (Courtesy of Bruce Davidson/Magnum Photos)

editorial representative for Farrar, Straus and Giroux at the time, first approached Gallimard, with no success. When he submitted *The Slave* to André Bay, the editor of the renowned *"Le Cabinet Cosmopolite"* at Éditions Stock, Bay didn't have a moment's hesitation. "André Bay answered right away," recalls Lottman. "He was an unusually perceptive reader. He saw immediately that these books had a new tone and a magical quality. There were three editors in the world—André Bay at Stock, Christoph Schlotterer at Hanser, and Lisa Morpurgo at Longanesi—who understood this instantly and, in spite of weak initial sales, remained committed to the entire work."[12] No doubt the quality of Singer's writings was obvious to these editors. "I was struck by its universal spirituality," said Bay later. "The power of these books lies in the fact that we feel at home in them. Isaac isn't a party leader. He's a great citizen of the world."[13]

He began receiving fan letters from around the world. "I am an Italian from Trieste, a professor of German literature interested in Mitteleuropa," wrote Claudio Magris modestly in German in 1966. "Your work," he went on, "has filled me with enthusiasm: it's been years since I've seen such a masterful art of storytelling. But you're more than a great storyteller. For me, my family and friends, you have become an everyday companion: we talk about Raizel, Dr. Fischelson, Rabbi Jonathan almost every day . . . perhaps because Trieste has something of your enchanted atmosphere."[14]

By the mid-sixties, Singer had joined PEN, whose members included John Steinbeck, Philip Roth, Erskine Caldwell, Saul Bellow, and William Styron. But he also faithfully renewed his membership to the Union of Yiddish Writers on East Broadway. Could he have even imagined all this in the days when he hugged the walls of the Warsaw Yiddish Writers' Club? Certainly not.

"In Poland in the late twenties," he said, "right up to the time vhen I came to America in 1935, the despair vhich I felt vas the greatest despair vhich I have ever felt. I could barely find enough to eat in those years in Poland. Who even speaks of literary efforts? . . . From so much despair, I could barely write a thing . . . But I vas sure, absolutely sure then, that it vas my destiny in life to become a big nobody."[15]

Magazines, book publishers, readings, lectures . . . The "big no-body" was in great demand. He was even asked to write children's stories. One of his translators, Elizabeth Shub, was an editor of children's books at Harper & Row, and she convinced him to try. To her great surprise, given his indifference to children, Isaac accepted. *Zlateh the Goat*, *The Fearsome Inn*, *A Tale of Three Wishes*, and *The Topsy-Turvy Emperor of China* (dedicated to André Bay's little boy, Nicolas) soon became classic children's books. Some of his stories were embellished by great illustrators, such as Maurice Sendak. Singer very much enjoyed writing these books. In 1979, he said:

> There are five hundred reasons why I began to write for children, but to save time, I will mention only ten of them.
>
> Number 1.   Children read books, not reviews. They don't give a hoot about the critics.
>
> Number 2.   Children don't read to find their identity.
>
> Number 3.   They don't read to free themselves of guilt, to quench their thirst for rebellion, or to get rid of alienation.
>
> Number 4.   They have no use for psychology.
>
> Number 5.   They detest sociology.
>
> Number 6.   They don't try to understand Kafka or *Finnegans Wake*.
>
> Number 7.   They still believe in God, the family, angels, devils, witches, goblins, logic, clarity, punctuation, and other such obsolete stuff.
>
> Number 8.   They love interesting stories, not commentary, guides, or footnotes.
>
> Number 9.   When a book is boring, they yawn openly, without any shame or fear of authority.
>
> Number 10. They don't expect their beloved writer to redeem humanity. Young as they are, they know that it is not in his power. Only the adults have such childish illusions.[16]

So almost by chance, Singer became a marvelous children's author. If he was so gifted for that genre as well, it was certainly, as André

Bay points out, "because the different aspects of his life, his character, his mind, and the traditions he had known, far from separating him from the genius peculiar to childhood, had actually contributed in constantly bringing him back to it."[17] As it turned out, the first National Book Award Isaac received was for *Zlateh the Goat* in 1970. Four years later, he was awarded the prize again, for *A Crown of Feathers*. He joined the ranks of that select group of writers—William Faulkner, Saul Bellow, John Updike, and Philip Roth—who were two-time recipients of this prestigious literary distinction.

"OUT, OUT—HE HAD BURST OUT, HE WAS IN THE WORLD OF REALITY . . ."

Achievement, recognition, success: it was hardly surprising that Singer felt fulfilled, a changed person. Those who had known him before, like his nephew Joseph, didn't recognize him. The others marveled at his wit and jokes. Nearing sixty, he was "between a sprite and a *bon papa*," says Dorothea Straus. In the American imagination, he was a kindly grandfather who was better than anyone at spinning out tales for all ages. At the end of his life, Henry Miller listed him as one of the "10 Greatest Writers of all Time" and called him a marvelous storyteller, adding that few "know so well how to sing, how to dance, or how to weep."[18] This was how he would be immortalized by the general public—not as a novelist or short-story writer, but as a teller of tales. Singer's masterstroke was to succeed in putting himself onstage like one of his protagonists, in simple and biblical lighting where mischievous spirits and dybbuks with foreign names flutter in the air, like a Chagall painting where "embracing lovers glide through a bright pink sky with a bearded violinist, while a goat on the roof and 'a dark-eyed angel' look on from afar."[19] Reality transfigured by the supernatural, where Isaac, having ably carved his own statue, became the frail guardian of this luscious, poetic folklore.

Of course, nothing was more irritating to his colleagues at the *Forward*. There he was the subject of endless criticism. Since they didn't like him, they accused him of being cold and distant when he dropped by the editorial offices. Isaac, on the other hand, told Robert Giroux that his *Forward* colleagues never said hello to him. Were they making him pay for his success? This seems plausible. We need only read Cynthia Ozick's short story "Envy; or, Yiddish in America" (1969) to get an idea of the jealousy and bitterness that troubled the small world of Yiddish authors at the time. In the person of Ostrover, a famous writer, Ozick had fun sketching a thinly veiled caricature of Singer. Two obscure pencil pushers, Edelshtein and Baumzweig, gravitate around him, both seething with spite and jealousy.

> Edelshtein's friendship with Baumzweig had a ferocious secret: it was moored entirely to their agreed hatred for the man they called *der chazer*. He was named Pig because of his extraordinarily white skin, like a tissue of pale ham, and also because in the last decade he had become unbelievably famous. When they did not call him Pig they called him *shed*—Devil. They also called him Yankee Doodle. His name was Yankel Ostrover, and he was a writer of stories . . .
>
> Though he wrote only in Yiddish, his fame was American, national, international. They considered him a "modern." Ostrover was free of the prison of Yiddish! Out, out—he had burst out, he was in the world of reality . . .
>
> And how had he begun? The same as anybody, a columnist for one of the Yiddish dailies, a humorist, a cheap fast article-writer, a squeezer-out of real-life tales. Like anybody else, he saved up a few dollars . . . Like anybody else, his literary gods were Chekhov and Tolstoy, Peretz and Sholem Aleichem. From this, how did he come to *The New Yorker*, to *Playboy*, to big lecture fees, invitations to Yale and M.I.T. and Vassar, to the Midwest, to Buenos Aires, to a literary agent, to a publisher on Madison Avenue?
>
> "He sleeps with the right translators," Paula said.[20]

Beyond bitterness and rivalry, there seemed to be a deeper misunderstanding between Singer and the Yiddish intellectual circles of his time. Irving Howe discussed this rift in *Commentary* as early as 1960. The Yiddish-speaking public, he writes, "tends to be a little puritanical in regard to sexual matters," and also tends to object to the fact that Singer "populates his novels with imps, with devils, with Satans, with seizures, epileptic fits, false Messiahs—all kinds of strange creatures that a nice Jewish mother wouldn't let into her house." He concludes that Yiddish readers have always been ambivalent about Isaac. On the one hand, they admire him; on the other, they recognize "that there's a very great spiritual distance between them and him."[21]

The writer who delighted the goyim disturbed his own people. But Isaac didn't care. He encouraged a young playwright who later encountered the same kind of difficulties. "Don't worry," he said. "They see me as a pornographer." He didn't care what a small coterie of envious people thought of his work. But why did Singer still seem agitated in spite of his success, torn between pride and self-hatred? The strange thing was, he referred to himself with the same nickname as the one used by his rivals in Cynthia Ozick's story. "I am a pig," he used to say. "I will go to Gehenna." Sometimes, he even signed his letters "the pig." This may have been partly a joke or self-mockery. But the word crops up too often to be ignored. Apparently he was repelled by something within himself. But what?

HIS PAST CATCHES UP WITH HIM

It is a "bitter truth" he hid deep inside. "When people meet me I am friendly. I make jokes; I cannot insult any human being. But let me tell you the bitter truth; I am in constant despair . . . because I see the lies and the treachery."[22] Treachery he himself was capable of. The treacherous way he had behaved with his family—his father, his brother, and especially his son—was a hidden source of guilt. And by the mid-fifties, his past was beginning to catch up with him.

In 1954, his sister, Hinde Esther, died in London. *In My Father's Court* reveals that Hinde Esther had been epileptic since childhood. She also suffered from serious anxiety attacks that later developed into a persecution complex. In spite of these problems and with virtually no encouragement from her parents, Hinde Esther succeeded in showing that she, too, had literary talent. She wrote two novels under her married name, Kreitman, *Der sheydim-tants* (*The Dance of Demons*) and *Brilyantn* (*Diamonds*), as well as a collection of short stories, *Yikhes* (*Lineages*). In the fifties, Hinde Esther was the only remaining tie Singer still had to his European past. However, between 1951 and 1954, her health deteriorated. Esther's son, Maurice Carr, wrote to Singer, telling him how they were faring. "Will you be passing through Europe? Then I hope you will visit my mother," he writes. "Meanwhile, I suggest you write to tell my mother that you will be visiting her, that is, if you really will be . . . Please, write to my mother soon because suspense is bad for her," he pleaded.[23] Carr was also one of Singer's translators. In the same letter he informed Isaac of his translation progress and repeatedly asked him for money for himself and his mother. No one knows how Isaac replied, but from his nephew's tone—reproaching him vehemently for his "absence of compassion"—it appears that Isaac turned a deaf ear.[24] Indeed, in July 1954, Carr wrote him the following grim words: "Dear Isaac, I have received your letter. As you do not want to have details on my mother's tragic life and death, I shall give you none."[25] In 1955, he wrote a note asking Isaac to contribute to the purchase of Esther's tombstone. Then he stopped writing for years—an eloquent, resentful silence.

That same year, 1955, another cause of guilt and anxiety resurfaced: Israel Zamir. This reddish-haired twenty-five-year-old young man who suddenly turned up for the second time in Isaac's life was none other than his son, the little boy of five Isaac had abandoned in prewar Warsaw. Brought up by his mother in the Beth Alpha kibbutz near Tel Aviv, Israel Zamir, after a twenty-year separation, wanted to meet the father he didn't know.

Israel hadn't heard from his father in years. Singer was an abstract idea to him. "I got used to the notion that he existed somewhere, as I got used to my own breathing," he later wrote. Singer sent news only occasionally. Every once in a while, he seemed suddenly to remember his son's existence and wrote to him. "He wanted to know how I was doing, who my friends were, and once he even asked if I 'had young ladies.' "[26]

In his correspondence, Isaac often expressed great feelings of affection that don't quite jibe with his behavior, as the following letter illustrates. Written in Hebrew and dated 1944, the letter makes no mention of events in his own life.

To my dear, beloved son!

Thank you very much for your letter. I'm so glad you're speaking, reading, and writing Hebrew. When I left for America, you were five years old. Now you're fourteen. I miss seeing you, talking and laughing with you very much. I have two pictures of you and when I look at them I miss you even more. As soon as the war is over, I'll try to come to Eretz-Israel, or you'll visit America. It's been a long time since I've written Hebrew. My beloved child, I love you very much. You're my only son and my soul is bound up with yours. I'm waiting for your letters. I want to know all the details. Do you like the kibbutz? Who are your friends? What do you read? How do you play in your free time? I don't want you to be sad for a moment. The victory over our enemies is approaching . . .

I kiss you with much love.

Your father,
Isaac.[27]

When he writes these tender words, Singer appears to believe the scenario he describes. Perhaps, at that point in time, he really did. Perhaps it contained the same truth as his works of fiction. Yet, as Israel Zamir notes, by 1944 Singer had already been "secretly" married to Alma for four years. "How could he still write, 'I'll come to see you when the war is over'? How could he say 'I love you'?" wonders Israel, sixty years later. Probably, once again, Isaac was both "here and there," sincere in his lies and duped by his own deceit. Probably, for a period of time, he genuinely wanted to get closer to his son. But discouraged by his mother, Israel's answers to his father's letters were cold and distant. In fact, he burned most of them. They were written in an old-fashioned Hebrew that embarrassed Israel. He was equally ashamed when he discovered Isaac's first novels. He felt, as many others did, that his father focused too much on sex and was too eager to put "nice yeshiva students into the beds of women who scorned religion." Worried that these books might fall into the hands of his fellow classmates at the kibbutz, he kept them hidden under his mattress.

Gradually, Singer's letters came less frequently. Occasionally for Gigi's birthday or Rosh Hashanah, the Jewish New Year, he sent a bicycle or a few dollars. Israel wondered if these gifts were tokens of love or of guilt. But he accepted them because he needed pocket money. He didn't feel any affection for his father, but as time went by, he wanted to meet him, not to judge him but out of curiosity.[28]

In 1955, Israel wrote to Isaac to tell him he was coming to New York in February. What a disaster! Isaac and Alma were dismayed. How would they deal with this stranger? Backed into a corner, Singer was terrified. "I was afraid of all the complications," he admitted to Israel years later. "You would have had to stay in the living room, and all kinds of women would call me. I'd have to apologize, explain, maybe lie."[29] Isaac had no desire to go over the past, no desire to justify his having left Runya. Moreover, the political climate was far from ideal. In the mid-1950s, in the middle of the McCarthy period, Isaac was frightened: his socialist son, fresh from a kibbutz, could get him into trouble. Did he have a choice? Could he simply refuse to welcome him? Alma said nothing; she insisted Isaac make up his own mind. And so after a twenty-year separation, filled with dread and anxiety, Isaac went to meet the stranger arriving at the port of New York in February 1955.

A TERRIFYING FACE-TO-FACE REUNION

The pier, the fog, the ship's delayed arrival, the crush of the crowds, a stressful reunion. We have two perspectives on this momentous occasion, two equally subjective points of view, the father's and the son's. Whom should we believe? In his account, *Journey to My Father*, Israel Zamir remembers that he was "overwhelmed" at the thought that he and his father were going to meet face to face. On the deck of the ship he roared the magic word "Father!" into the wind. Then as the ship

was about to dock, he was filled with apprehension. What kind of feelings could a man have for his twenty-five-year-old son after a twenty-
year absence? Would they have anything in common after so many
years? Israel went through immigration and disembarked. He looked
all around but saw no one. "Why don't you go to Information and ask
them to page your father?" a woman suggested. Israel rejected the
idea. He was too nervous. He wanted to meet his father quietly. Suddenly, he spotted a fair-skinned man with reddish hair who winked at
him. "Mr. Singer?" The man didn't reply immediately, leaving things
ambiguous, but Israel understood he had mistaken someone else for
his father. A botched reunion, a mistaken identity: not a very emotionally fulfilling arrival. A cold wind blew outside. It was raining. New
York looked ugly to him. It was only when he left the port that he saw
people crowded behind a barricade:

> As I approached them, I identified my father. This time it felt
> right; I knew it was him. He was standing off to the side of the
> street and looking at me closely, restrained. That had to be the
> way he looked, I was sure; this man's medium height and light-
> skinned face seemed to fit what I thought corresponded to my
> father's features. His short chin ended in a tiny knob; his eye-
> glasses, even the coat and felt hat he wore, seemed right to me.
> Not allowing myself to show my excitement, I tried to look
> calm and slowly passed him by.
>
> "Gigi?" the man called out. I hadn't heard my childhood
> name in so many years!
>
> "Yes," I responded quickly, like a soldier in basic training.
> We shook hands. He kissed me. We stood there, embarrassed
> and silent. All my life, I had imagined this encounter with my
> father. There we both were, and I was choked up and ex-
> hausted, unable to say a thing. We stood in silence for a long
> while until he decided to hail a cab. I felt as though I was com-
> ing out of a deep sleep.[30]

Isaac described the scene in the short story "The Son," revealing ir-
ritation rather than confusion. The ship is late. Israel had sent him a

photograph, but it was blurry. Singer paces around and worries. Only then does he realize he has no clear image of what his son looks like. Tall? Short? He thinks of Runya again, the idealist who dreamed of "permanent revolution." What foolishness! The arrival of his son pushed him back "to an epoch . . . already belonging to eternity." He looks around him. Amid the joy and excitement of all those who had come to meet their relatives, Singer remains an "outsider." This son emerging out of the past did not fit into his present life; he "had no room for him, no bed, no money, no time." Ironically, he too mistakes someone else for Israel. He is about to call out "Gigi" to a young man when he sees a woman, probably his girlfriend, rush over to him . . . Then, finally, Singer sees his son and remains paralyzed. "Instead of running to him immediately, I stood and gaped . . . He took after me, but I recognized traits of his mother—the other half that could never blend with mine. Even in him, the product, our contrary traits had no harmony. The mother's lips did not pair with the father's chin . . . We kissed and his stubble rubbed my cheeks like a potato grater. He was strange to me . . ."[31]

Strange? It is true that Israel, a stocky, heavyset man with thick reddish eyebrows, doesn't at all resemble his father. But when he looks at you, even today, you feel Singer's eyes gazing into yours. The same limpid, metallic ray of blue light. Isaac was not moved. When they arrived home—Isaac still lived at the corner of Central Park West and 101st Street—Israel noticed that the dining room was full of books and that newspapers covered the dining room table. In the living room, Alma had set up a folding bed, bought especially for him. She gave him a warm welcome, but her very presence was a shock for him. "Imagine," he said fifty years later, "it was only in 1955, when I took the initiative to see my father in America, that I—and my mother!—discovered Alma's existence!"[32]

The clash between father and son was actually great. It was almost a clash of civilizations. On the one hand was a young man eager to talk, a Zionist, a fervent Socialist, who spoke very little Yiddish. On the other, a conservative—Zamir said reactionary—man of fifty whose

Hebrew seemed to come straight out of the Talmud . . . Singer versus Zamir. Their incompatibility is not surprising. Isaac made a half-hearted effort by taking his son to the Metropolitan Museum of Art, but after twenty minutes, he became impatient. "Let's go back home," he said. "I've got lots of work to do." Soon he was buried in his papers and never looked up. The awkwardness grew. "I didn't know what to call him—certainly not Father or Dad," says Israel Zamir. "So I called him, 'Listen'—at least that's how I began all my sentences." But with every "listen," Israel had the feeling he was disturbing him. Furthermore, Singer was dreadfully stingy with him. A dollar a day was all he gave him. "Within a few days," he writes, "it became obvious that my father wouldn't have time for me. He didn't know what to do with me. He had no time and no money."[33]

"SINGER WAS NOT A FAMILY MAN"

Though this first meeting was a fiasco, the barrier separating the two men eventually came down. After this first trip, Israel Zamir returned to New York as his kibbutz's youth representative. Singer made several trips to Israel. But Israel Zamir really succeeded in getting close to his father only when he started translating Isaac's books into Hebrew, touching on what Singer truly cared about: his literary creations. Singer admitted as much quite clearly: "My stories are my children."

Fifty years later, the wounded young man of the 1950s is the father of four children and the grandfather of five. A journalist, a member of the editorial committee of the Maariv group, Israel Zamir still lives in the same Beth Alpha kibbutz, two hours from Tel Aviv. His mother, Runya, had remarried in 1945; her husband was a Jerusalem business-man. She died in the late 1980s without ever seeing Isaac again, filled with hatred for him until the end. What about Israel? Has he come to accept, if not understand, his father's behavior? He responds to every question with a fatalistic shrug. "Singer was not a family man," he says matter-of-factly, the way he might say, "Singer had big ears" or "Singer had a very pale complexion."

Perhaps such self-control and reticence conceal an open wound. Yet Israel seems sincere when he tries to find excuses for his father. "Isn't such fierce independence typical of artists? Wasn't he lost himself, this man who spoke Yiddish to birds?" He even forgives his stinginess. He had "trouble adjusting to his life of recent comfort after so many years of financial straits, when he literally didn't have a cent in his pocket and had to calculate everything very carefully . . . In his early American years, he often thought of committing suicide."[34] It was difficult for him to get used to his new financial situation.

The Singer of the sixties is hard to characterize. On the positive side is Isaac the charmer, delighting his audiences and watching fan letters pile up. His correspondence of the period includes genuine declarations of love. A woman he doesn't know wishes him a happy birthday; a reader from New York named Mary Brancroft congratulates him for being "so wonderfully modest and unpretentious."[35] On the less positive side is the egocentric Bashevis who can't make the effort to welcome the son he has not seen in twenty years. A great mind sustained by the Kabbalah and Spinoza, yet capable of base pettiness, reproaching his son for weighing 150 pounds or leaving food on his plate. Isaac versus Bashevis. Public persona versus private citizen. This duality always persisted. It was just the way Singer was. He could be charming and witty so long as nothing and no one interfered with his "system," coming between him and his books.

Such boundless egoism may seem infantile. But at least Singer was sincere and frank. There was no pretense or self-deception; he refused to become mired in the sham of family bonds. For someone like Isaac, steeped in the Talmud and the Torah, this "business of the son"— desertion and the son's return—couldn't have been a simple matter. Its symbolic dimension is so strong that it borders on the sacred. Hence, all his life, he responded with absolute silence whenever anyone broached the subject. Yet he never changed his mind. Back in Poland, he had already decided that having a family was a nuisance. Children were traps, terrifying burdens, a constant responsibility limiting one's freedom. Singer did everything he could to avoid such ties. He remained faithful to this decision throughout his life, recalling

St.-John Perse's line: "To leave, on the honor of the living." The hero is often the person who has egoism enough to take charge and be true to himself, accepting his own weaknesses, cowardliness, and unresolved conflicts. In that respect, Isaac was a free spirit, in the fullest, most demanding sense of the term. Singer versus Singer.

NINE

"How Long Can a Man Be Surprised?
How Long Can a Man Be Happy?"

DVORAH COULDN'T GET OVER IT. Isaac's words were a slap in the face, definitive: "You're not coming." How could this be? He was going to Stockholm, to claim the Nobel Prize, and she wouldn't be going. Impossible. A short while earlier, Isaac had been in a marvelous mood. At home, he sat hunched in a chair, scribbling in a notebook on his knee, writing his Nobel speech. After half an hour, he proclaimed, "Yes, I have it." Happy and relaxed, Isaac and his young assistant went for a walk on Seventh Avenue, as was their habit. Passing a luggage store, Dvorah said, almost without thinking, "I better pick up a few new suitcases for the trip." Isaac shot back, a quick phrase like a blow to the head, "You're not coming."

Dvorah couldn't get over it. To think he could be this callous, offhandedly telling her she was persona non grata. "I was stunned," she wrote years later. "I felt so much a part of this victory, it was as if a member of my own family was getting married and I wasn't invited."[1] On that autumn day in 1978, the young woman lost her bearings. Could she have been mistaken about the man she so loved and admired? How could the same man who kept calling her his "prize," his "little sweet daughter," his "embryo," betray her so casually?[2] The man who had pleaded with her three years earlier, "I vant you should tell me everything about your whole life from beginning to end, right naah!"[3]

ISAAC'S PERSONAL CHAUFFEUR

The story behind their meeting is an odd one. Singer first met Dvorah in September 1975, shortly before he began teaching a creative writing course at Bard College, in Annandale-on-Hudson. He was seventy-one; she was twenty-one. At the time, Dvorah was married to Abraham Menashe, a photojournalist. She had just lost her mother under tragic circumstances but kept in mind her last words, prompted by an article about Singer in *The New York Times*, "Why don't you go knock on this Isaac Singer's door? I think he could help you." Not long after her mother's death, on a day when she felt particularly dejected and vulnerable, Dvorah followed her advice. In late August 1975, she sent Isaac a touching, childlike note for the Jewish New Year. She had made a card herself with a drawing in black ink of something that looked like a couple under a wedding canopy. "To our Dear Isaac Singer. It was overwhelming and joyous news for me to learn that you will be teaching at Bard College . . . If you allow me to audit your course on creative writing, I can offer to drive you every Tuesday. Your heritage and love of Yiddishkeit is very dear and close to my heart."[4]

He accepted her offer. For six months, Dvorah became Isaac's personal chauffeur. After that, she became his secretary, companion, messenger, and confidante—and one of his editors, under the guidance of *The New Yorker*'s eminent Rachel McKenzie. Above all, in the last fifteen years of his life, she was his close friend; there was a sincere bond between them, the kind that sometimes exists in relationships with great age differences. He was a "master of charm," writes Dvorah in her memoir. "At seventy-one, he was agile, productive, full of vigor and imagination." Singer often repeated that without Dvorah he would be completely *farblondzhet* (lost). "You lead me like a dog on a leash," he said to her, "but I cannot help it."[5]

ALMA PREFERRED NEVER TO MENTION HER NAME

From 1976 on, Dvorah did everything for Isaac. While Alma was at work, Dvorah answered the mail and tidied up Isaac's indescribably messy "chaos room," with its piles of yellowed papers, old issues of the *Forward*, and pages of manuscripts he couldn't bring himself to throw out. Isaac often joked, but with pride, "I can say I have accomplished vone thing in my life, my chaos has reached perfection!"[6] Dvorah typed English translations from his dictation, revised his *New Yorker* galleys with him, and helped him "polish" his short stories until they "shined."[7] She adjusted to his frenzied work pace and accompanied him to his lectures, seminars, and countless readings. She lunched with him at his favorite vegetarian coffee shops—the Éclair Café or the Famous Dairy Restaurant on Seventy-second Street, Three Brothers on Eighty-eighth Street, Tibbs on Seventy-fourth Street. She ate mainly to reassure him, she says. "Probably because of the hardships he had experienced in his youth, he was terribly anguished at the thought that I might be hungry." Afterward they would walk briskly to Riverside Park or Central Park. "Fifty or sixty blocks, full speed ahead with his head lowered. These were the only moments when he would let his mind wander," Dvorah recalls. "Otherwise, Isaac never wasted a minute. 'Vhere vere vee?' he asked when we got back to work. He would plunge back into his stories immediately. His concentration was such that there was something like a halo around his desk."[8]

As they strode down the city streets or fed the pigeons, Isaac told her about his Poland of the past. Dvorah was captivated. "I wouldn't say he was really a womanizer," she notes nearly thirty years later. "That notion, played up by all the commentators, reminds me of Mark Twain's joke, 'Rumors of my death are greatly exaggerated.' I was struck by his respect for women. His way of asking permission before kissing their hand. A very Old World sensitivity. Yes, he was immensely respectful of women. The American-style permissive society drove him crazy."[9]

Isaac was fascinated by Dvorah, her youth, her freshness, her ingenuousness. He was also touched by her extreme devotion. "He liked people who were capable of giving up everything for him," says Dvorah, "as Alma had." Had Dvorah ever considered giving everything up for him? She assured me she hadn't. Sitting in her West End Avenue apartment thirty years later, now the wife of Rabbi Joseph

Telushkin, with whom she has had three children, this elegant brunette laughed. "No, we never considered living together. First of all, I was married. When I divorced I was thirty and he was eighty and already ill. I married Joseph two years later."[10]

In the late seventies, Dvorah occupied such a significant place in Isaac's life that Alma preferred never to mention her name. In the summer, in Wengen, Dvorah would phone from New York almost every evening. "Alma chose to look the other way. She called her 'Isaac's secretary,' " says Marie-Pierre Bay.[11] Isaac may have even considered a divorce at the time. It is rumored that the three—Dvorah, Alma, and Isaac—discussed the possibility of divorce. Singer, like Borges, may have been tempted to yield to his late autumn passion to prove to himself that he was still alive. But in the end Isaac couldn't bring himself to leave Alma.

It is hard to distinguish truth from falsehood. Which of the two versions is reliable? We may never know and, in the end, the difference may not be so crucial. More interesting is how Singer, having fallen in love, adapted to the situation. He often said, "Vith vone flame, vone could light many candles," a roundabout way of referring to the Talmud and the idea that if one individual knew a sacred text, he could teach it to many without diminishing his own knowledge.[12] To Isaac, loving several women didn't mean that his love for each was diminished. Such was his belief, although no doubt it was difficult for the women involved to share. This relationship certainly could not have been easy on him, either. Trapped in a seemingly inextricable dilemma of his own making, Isaac managed to disentangle himself through ruse or escape. "Come over quickly," he said to Roger Straus on the phone one day. "Come now: they're both out." Straus rushed over to Isaac's and was handed a carton of archives. "They're fighting over who will get my papers after I die," Isaac explained. "Take these and above all don't tell anyone."[13]

The Nobel Prize posed a similar quandary. Singer obviously couldn't bring two women to Stockholm. So he simply avoided making the decision. Alma wanted to invite two of her friends, Sally and

Mildred: How could he turn her down? "The Nobel Committee or whoever is in charge of this whole business only allows seven guests to each writer. Vhat can I do? Alma has already promised her cronies there from Miami: this Sally and Mildred. And I have not the *kovekh* (strength) to fight vith them,"[14] he explained, embarrassed, as they stood in front of the luggage store on Seventh Avenue. This was the excuse he gave Dvorah—at least when she herself broached the subject. Until then he had been careful to avoid it.

AFTER 10:30 WE HAD TO SURRENDER

The whole business of the Nobel Prize had taken Isaac completely by surprise. The day the prize was announced, on October 5, 1978, he and Alma were in Miami Beach, staying in the condominium they had bought in 1973 and where they regularly went for vacation.[15] Isaac had gone out for a morning walk and then went to meet Alma for breakfast. But Alma was late. She had just received a telephone call: Isaac was being awarded the Nobel Prize! "Are you sure it's true?" Singer asked. "It must be a mistake. They must be confusing it with a nomination for a Nobel Prize. In any case, let's eat breakfast. What do you think—we can stop eating because of happiness?"

A few days later, a letter written by Alma describes their disbelief: "We were in Miami when the news came and we were taken completely by surprise, so much so that we disbelieved the first morning calls that people made to us who heard it at the *Today Show* at 8 a.m. But then after 10:30, when the television crews and the telephone calls from the *Jewish Daily Forward* came, we surrendered."[16]

The Nobel Prize? Isaac had stopped believing it was possible. True, he had dreamt of it. For many years, he had probably applied to himself the well-known maxim of people who thirst for power: always think of it, never speak of it. But by 1978, he had given up thinking about it. When the United States celebrated its bicentennial two years earlier, the Nobel Prize jury, eager to award the prize to an American, had chosen Saul Bellow. Bellow, his enemy of thirty years! All of Isaac's hopes were dashed that day. After that, why would the

Nobel Academy be inclined to give the award to a writer akin to Bellow? Why would it honor another American Jew two years later? Moreover, as Jean-Louis Ezine pointed out in *Les Nouvelles littéraires*, Singer's name wasn't among those mentioned that year. "Breaking the sacrosanct duty to preserve secrecy, one of the Swedish jury members had even publicly backed, in a Stockholm newspaper, the candidacy of the eternal potential Nobel Prize–winner Graham Greene. The laurels and the 725,000 kronor seemed promised to him this year. To him or to the British writer Lawrence Durrell. Or else to his California friend Henry Miller, the English writer Doris Lessing, the Turkish writer Yachar Kemal, or the French writer Simone de Beauvoir. But of Singer, not a word."[17]

In fact, Singer had long been wary of nursing futile hopes. Ten years before they honored Bellow, the Nobel committee had awarded literature prizes to the Israeli writer Shmuel Yosef Agnon and the poet Nelly Sachs. Israel Zamir was with his father in 1966 when they heard the news. "My father seemed surprised and a little sad," Zamir recalls. "He tried to restrain his emotions, but his hands trembled and revealed what he was feeling. For years he had been cited as a candidate for the prize." Isaac "seemed resigned to never being one of the winners himself. His own chances for the desired prize were nil or, as he put it, he was 'a withered noble Nobel blossom.' "[18]

What Singer didn't know was that he benefited from very active supporters in Stockholm. One of the members of the Swedish Academy, Knut Ahnlund, had been a passionate admirer of his work since the early seventies. Writer, biographer,[19] literary critic in *Svenska Dagbadett*, Ahnlund discovered Isaac in English in 1975, becoming almost obsessed with him. In 1977, he went to New York to meet Singer in order to better introduce him to his fellow academicians. He returned captivated by this "witty, piquant, quick" man, "the most intelligent person I had ever met," he says. That year, he wrote an article titled "The Swan Song of the Yiddish Language," published in *Artes*, the journal of the Swedish Academy. In this essay, he stresses what an "immense storyteller Singer is. A storyteller of genius, from the first to the last line, with, behind him, the entire Polish Jewish supernatural tradition of the *shtetl*." Ahnlund's admiration was infectious. Soon the academy's permanent secretary, Lars Gyllensten, was won over as well. "The timing was good. Gyllensten was already convinced that a separate case had to be made for minority languages and dying languages," says Ahnlund. "The deliberation was short and the decision unanimous. Everyone at the academy had become passionately enthusiastic about Singer."[20]

"MAZEL TOV!"

"Mazel tov!" Dvorah exclaimed when Isaac called her from Miami. She had been trying to reach him for hours, but his phone had been constantly busy. She wanted to tell him that her answering machine was overloaded with messages and that telegrams were flowing in, from Henry Miller; Yitzhak Navon, the president of Israel; Teddy Kollek, the mayor of Jerusalem; from *Time, Newsweek,* and from all the Jewish organizations in the world. "Do you know that the President, Carter, called me?" Isaac said. "It seems he did not know that it vas Yom Kippur. But I answered the phone anyhow. I didn't mention a vord, God forbid."[21]

In October 1978, *The New York Times* and *The Washington Post* were on strike. In the meantime, Singer made the front pages of other newspapers—sometimes as an American, sometimes as a Pole. He was interviewed on the radio and invited to be a guest on the *Dick Cavett Show.* When *The New York Times* resumed publication in November, Christopher Lehmann-Haupt praised the way Isaac had made the East European Jew "an exemplar of the suffering modern man who has been exiled from his divine inheritance." Situating Singer in "the tradition of such Yiddish storytelling masters as Mendele, Aleichem, Peretz and Asch," he noted that "any writer who can command a following in such disparate publications as the *Jewish Daily Forward, The New Yorker, Commentary* and *Playboy* can scarcely be accused of cultural parochialism."[22] *The Times* printed a few lines of Singer's work in Yiddish for the occasion.

This simple idea, which emerges as a recurrent theme in all the commentaries—Singer as a universal writer and not the standard-bearer of the Jewish community—is probably, when all is said and done, what most annoyed American Yiddishists. They probably felt that, once again, something was overtaking them and escaping from them. Yet this was the first time in the history of the Nobel Prize that a Yiddish writer had been given the literature award, the first time this minority language had been greatly honored outside the Jewish world. At the *Forward*, where the editor in chief, Simon Weber, gave a big party in Isaac's honor and expressed his pride in Isaac and his newspaper, Isaac said, "I am not the only winner of the Prize. I share it with all my readers and with all lovers of the Yiddish language."[23]

However, in some sectors, reaction to the news was cool. *The Morgn-frayhayt* wrote that though the academy's choice was "very important" and "positive, . . . in the Yiddish writers' world, I. Bashevis-Singer has been and will be evaluated not at all unanimously with praise because of the sexual element and the reactionary mysticism of his writing—which definitely made his work into 'best sellers' in English and other languages." The author mentions other "greater Yiddish writers," such as Elye Shekhtman and Avrom Sutskever. One of his fellow writers accuses the *Forward* of making Singer into a "cult," while the writer Chaim Grade, out of bitterness, no doubt, goes so far as to call this Nobel Prize a "great tragedy for the Jewish people."[24]

Fortunately, Isaac had no time for such backbiting. When he returned to New York, he was assaulted by journalists, universities, and the media. He couldn't write a single line. It was all incredibly time-consuming, not to mention that he was asked the same questions over and over: "Are you surprised? Are you happy?" This went on for days. So he found a sure-fire way of throwing off his interviewer. Since he had no desire to go on at length about happiness, he simply replied with his own questions. "How long can a man be surprised? How long can a man be happy?"[25]

THE NOBEL PRIZE WINNER AND THE CLEANING WOMAN

On December 6, 1978, a crowd of reporters, TV cameramen, and photographers waited at the Stockholm airport. As soon as Singer disembarked from the plane, accompanied by Alma and her guests—as well as Roger and Dorothea Straus, Robert Giroux, Simon Weber, and Paul Kresh—he was bombarded with questions: "Mr. Singer, why do you still write in Yiddish?" "Which writers influenced you most?" "Mr. Singer, Pope Paul VI just died. Are you happy that the new pope is a Pole?" "Are you a vegetarian for religious or health reasons?" This last question was one to which Isaac replied, deadpan, "It is the health of the chickens with which I am concerned, not my own."

All the members in his group were in boots and bundled up as if they were going on an expedition to the North Pole. Singer wore his usual old overcoat and felt hat, and carried his black umbrella—the trappings that made Americans think he looked so European. His pale skin, his frail demeanor—he was seventy-four—may have made people think of him as weak and elderly. But his twinkling blue eyes testified to the contrary. He was clearly delighted to be photographed. He paid tribute to Joshua, his brother and mentor—in private he had said to Dvorah Telushkin, "It is my brother who should have gotten the Prize, not I."[26] He teased the journalists. "Why do you ask so many questions about my life?" he said, acting surprised. The work is what counts. "When I am hungry, do I want to read a biography of the baker?"

At the Grand Hotel in Stockholm, where he was given the celebrity suite, Singer continued to surprise his entourage. In theory there was no time for additions to his schedule, between the luncheons, lectures, press conferences, receptions, and dress rehearsals for the gala reception. Yet Isaac's Swedish editor, Dorotea Bromberg, recounts how he still managed to bring about the kind of meeting only he was capable of. Dorotea was twenty-four years old. Her family, Polish Jewish immigrants who had moved to Sweden eight years earlier with humble resources, had founded a small publishing house, Brombergs Förlag. In 1978, they had put out two of Singer's books in Swedish, *The Magician from Lublin* and *Gimpel the Fool*. Dorotea had an appointment for a cup of coffee with Singer at the Grand Hotel but felt "terribly nervous":

> The publishing house was very young, and so was I. There was the aura of this Nobel Prize winner who was already known as a great writer in America. I said to myself, "When he sees who

his Swedish publisher is, he'll change houses." In the hotel lobby, there was a throng of journalists around a little fellow, Isaac. They were all excited and showered him with questions. But Singer didn't reply. He was completely absorbed with a cleaning woman from the Grand Hotel who had carried *The Magician of Lublin* around all day in hopes of seeing him and asking him for a dedication. Isaac said to her, "Of course, I'll sign your book, but first, tell me about yourself." She was Finnish, divorced, and getting ready to return to her own country. This was the starting point for a twenty-minute conversation—about her private life—while all the journalists tugged at his sleeve. That was typical Singer. He always wanted to know everything, even the most intimate details. And he always succeeded. He knew how to ask questions without making people ill at ease. He knew how to access the mysterious areas of the soul where modesty and immodesty meet, perhaps because his interest was sincere. He was truly curious about human nature. After twenty minutes—which seemed to me like an eternity—I felt obliged to get him and rescue him from the pack of journalists. We had coffee together and within five minutes had become friends for life.[27]

A NOBEL UNLIKE ANY OTHER

A few days later, everything was ready for the ceremonies. Israel Zamir—who was covering the event for his paper—stayed at the Grand Hotel as well. André and Marie-Pierre Bay came from Paris with their little boy, Nicolas. Alma, radiant in her cream-colored dress, seemed fulfilled. As for Singer, he glowed with happiness in the overly large tails he had rented for the occasion. As he got dressed, he kept losing things and mumbling, as if a spectator of himself, "What a fuss! What a business! You would think the Day of Judgment had come!"[28]

On December 8, the procession of audience and officials filed into the hall for his address to the academy. With his rosy cheeks and shiny bald head, Singer looked on, impassive. He had, as Dorothea Straus puts it, the equanimity of someone "who never forgets who he is and from where he comes."[29]

This was true. Isaac began his speech in Yiddish, an astonishing thing to do in this setting. The venerable hall of the academy, this temple of knowledge and civilization, resonated strangely from the millions of silenced voices:

"The high honor bestowed on me by the Swedish Academy is also a recognition of the Yiddish language—a language of exile, without a land, without frontiers, not supported by any government, a language which possesses no words for weapons, ammunition, military exercises, war tactics; a language that was despised by both gentiles and emancipated Jews." The audience sat in mute astonishment. Most of the guests didn't understand Yiddish and let themselves be lulled by the sonority of the language. Singer described his childhood in Poland and the Jewish ghetto as

a great experiment in peace, in self-discipline and in humanism . . . In our home and in many other homes the eternal questions were more actual than the latest news in the Yiddish newspaper. In spite of all the disenchantments and all my skepticism I believe that the nations can learn much from those Jews, their way of thinking, their way of bringing up children, their finding happiness where others see nothing but misery and humiliation . . . There is a quiet humor in Yiddish and a gratitude for every day of life, every crumb of success, each encounter of love. The Yiddish mentality is not haughty. It does not take victory for granted. It does not demand and command but it muddles through, sneaks by, smuggles itself amidst the powers of destruction, knowing somewhere that God's plan for Creation is still at the very beginning . . . In a figurative way, Yiddish is the wise and humble language of us all, the idiom of frightened and hopeful humanity.[30]

We are reminded of Kafka: in "An Introductory Talk on the Yiddish Language," he told his Prague audience that they understood more Yiddish than they thought.

After these words of praise for his native tongue, Isaac switched to English and expressed his faith in God and literature. But on the evening of December 10, during the formal banquet in the presence of the royal family, he returned to the issue of language on a more humorous note. He explained that he had always written in Yiddish because his stories were about ghosts, demons, and imps, and nothing was better suited for this purpose than a dying language. And also, he said, because he believed in resurrection and that when the millions of Yiddish-speaking dead woke up, their first question would be, "What's the latest Yiddish book?"[31]

There are countless other anecdotes about Singer's Nobel Prize. He is described as a kind of Charlie Chaplin, unconventional and touching, standing when he was supposed to sit and vice versa, walking and joking on the arm of a princess twice as tall as he. They say that at the end of the ceremony, he forgot to take his award check and ran back to fetch it. Singer was an unusually memorable prizewinner. "An historic event," said the permanent secretary, Lars Gyllensten, to Robert Giroux. "I don't doubt it," the latter answered. "It's certainly the first time a laureate spoke in Yiddish." "No, no," protested Gyllensten. "That's not what I mean. I've been secretary of this academy for years and it's the first time I've seen members laugh!"[32]

A Nobel unlike any other—this is also Knut Ahnlund's memory of the event. "The prize had an exceptional impact that year," he says. Dorotea Bromberg agrees. "In November and December 1978 alone, we sold 150,000 copies of *The Magician of Lublin*. Today, Singer sells over three million copies. This is enormous for this small country. There is no Swedish household that doesn't have a book by Isaac."[33]

"A RIVER OF HUMANITY"

Four days later, on December 14, 1978, Isaac and Alma left Stockholm for Paris, where other festivities awaited him. André and Marie-Pierre Bay had organized a party at Stock, on the Left Bank. On Friday evening, Isaac appeared on the prestigious literary talk show *Apostrophes*. The following day, he had lunch in the well-known

Paris delicatessen Jo Goldenberg, on the Rue des Rosiers. But the thing that struck Singer most during his stay in France was the homage paid to him on Sunday at the Sorbonne. Rarely had anyone witnessed a crowd so eager to enter the university. On December 17, people were nearly coming to blows at the entrance on Rue de la Sorbonne. A closed-circuit television had to be installed for the crowd outside.

The French academician Jean d'Ormesson, director of the newspaper *Le Figaro*, presided over the session. André Bay had wanted him to be present, because two years earlier, d'Ormesson had discovered Singer and had since become an ardent admirer, calling him an "immense writer." D'Ormesson had been ill, bedridden and bored, so he had reached for one of the many unread books he received every day. It happened to be Isaac Bashevis Singer's *A Crown of Feathers*. "No one had recommended this book to me. What a delight!" d'Ormesson recalled. "The title was unfamiliar and, to tell the truth, so was the writer. So I read *A Crown of Feathers*. And I was dazzled."

D'Ormesson proclaimed his admiration in the pages of *Le Figaro*, in an article titled "A River of Humanity." The article ended with the appeal, "Read Singer; you will not regret it." He expressed his admiration:

> Isaac Singer tells stories with a biblical simplicity. They dramatize the plight of poor people, often emigrants, slightly seedy Jewish intellectuals, students, artists, women in love, rabbis, and a few demons or crafty spirits. The *nouveau roman*, psychoanalysis, the baroque, and other refinements that thrive here seem to have made no mark on Singer's world. Nor can his style be called realism or naturalism, and it certainly does not dwell on the sordid. He depicts daily life, but illuminated from the inside from frequent contact with the sacred books ... there is not a single superfluous word, or useless description. A boundless love for living beings, a disarming humor, a keen sense of truth's infinite complexity and, above all, a sovereign, and to my mind very moving, simplicity. That, in a few words, sums up *A Crown of Feathers*.[34]

Years later, d'Ormesson recalled, "When the article appeared, I was the laughingstock of Paris. All my friends said to me, 'Where have you been? He's going to get the Nobel Prize, everyone knows him.' I discovered that people like Henry Miller and Edmund Wilson had long been ranking Singer among the greatest writers . . . Still, in 1978, when he was awarded the prize, Singer remembered that article. He wanted me to introduce him at the Sorbonne. It leads you to conclude that innocence is almost always rewarded."[35]

D'Ormesson remembers Singer as a "kindly, charming, very modest" man. Isaac was delighted with their encounter. The actor François Perier read selections from his writing, including "The Chimney Sweep." Singer kept and cherished a little handwritten card in Yiddish congratulating him for expressing the soul of a people. It had been given to him that afternoon by the pianist Arthur Rubinstein and was signed by Marc Chagall.

A PROFOUND MODESTY

With few exceptions—*L'Arche*, for example, in the Jewish press—this Nobel Prize was particularly well received in France.[36] *Le Monde* published an article the day the prize was announced and a second three-column article on October 15. Edgar Reichmann, one of the first literary critics to have championed Singer since the publication of his very first translations, mentioned "the hidden despair behind the politeness of humor" as well as the "tragic and elegant distance that is part of the tradition of Yiddish literature from Sholem Aleichem and Peretz to Mendel Mann and Babel."[37] *Le Figaro* ran an exclusive interview with a headline across its entire last page, "A Patriarch in New York." At Stock, everyone was jubilant. André Bay—who had published twelve Singer titles by 1978 under his imprint, Le Cabinet Cosmopolite—could congratulate himself on his judgment and patience. In a letter to Isaac in February 1979, he wrote, "Everyone in Paris and in France is reading Singer. In the bookstores around us, the books are snatched up as soon as they arrive. I've never seen anything like it."

The only place where the prize had no immediate effect was Poland. Except for one short story published in 1977, none of Singer's works existed in translation prior to 1978. Still, the prize did pique the Poles' curiosity about a Polish-born Nobel laureate whom almost no one had heard of. Elsewhere, in France, Sweden, Italy, and Japan, Isaac attained great fame. Yet he remained unaffected. If there was one thing he despised, it was self-aggrandizement. He never tried to be anyone but who he was. Before leaving Paris, Isaac and Alma had lunch at La Closerie des Lilas, with the Bays; Michelle Lapautre, his agent in France; and her husband, René. Sartre and Simone de Beauvoir were seated at a nearby table. André Bay offered to make the necessary introductions, but Isaac adamantly refused. Little did he know that, several days later, in the magazine *Le Nouvel Observateur*, Simone de Beauvoir would announce that she was enjoying discovering his work. Meanwhile, it is a telling anecdote. Why did Singer refuse to meet them? Was he embarrassed because Sartre had turned down the Nobel Prize several years earlier? Was it ideological, a "wariness" of the Left Bank intellectuals? No, the reason was probably humility. "Singer wasn't the least bit snobbish," remarks Herbert Lottman. "He never would have wanted to meet Sartre just to say he had shaken hands with him. And he was also shy, a trait linked to his past. He felt he couldn't really mix with the socially prominent."[38]

The splendors of Stockholm, the honors—Isaac let none of these change his life. Even the success of *Shosha*, which Farrar, Straus and Giroux published immediately after his Nobel Prize and which received enormous media coverage, left him unfazed. He still dressed in the same old-fashioned way. He still haunted the same Upper West Side luncheonettes—his "greasy spoon" restaurants, as Roger Straus called them. He still asked for boiled potatoes when he was taken to elegant restaurants at his hosts' insistence. Alma, on the other hand, would have been glad to improve her social standing. She gave lectures at her ladies' club and even thought about writing her memoirs. All of this tired Isaac. It seemed laughable. He kept repeating to anyone who would listen, "Yesterday I was a Yiddish writer, today I'm a Nobel Laureate, tomorrow I'll be a Yiddish writer."[39]

As for the "two Singers," they were still present. Dvorah Telushkin notes as much in her memoir: It was as though his face were divided in two. The upper half radiated light and serenity, while the lower half seemed twisted with anguish. What was he so frightened of? she wondered. When he returned home, Singer showed her his heavy gold medal and his Nobel "diploma." He also showed her a black-and-white photograph of himself receiving the Nobel Prize from the king of Sweden. As he looked at the photo, he commented, "I look like a frightened Jew, vhich is vhat I am echtually."[40]

THE GHOSTS OF THE HOLOCAUST

When he received the Nobel Prize, Singer was repeatedly asked why he had never written about the Holocaust. This reproach is ill founded. True, Isaac had always refused to tackle head-on a trauma he hadn't personally lived through. But traces of the Holocaust were ever present in the bruised souls and memories he wrote about in the 1970s. This is the case, for instance, in *Enemies, A Love Story*, published by Farrar, Straus and Giroux in 1972. *Enemies* marks a turning point in Singer's work. The setting and the period are no longer the same. This is Isaac's first novel set in the United States after the war. The protagonist, Herman Broder, has lost his family in the camps and escaped death by hiding in a hayloft. He now lives in Brooklyn with his second wife, Yadwiga, the Polish peasant woman who saved his life, but marriage doesn't prevent him from having an affair with the beautiful Masha. Then his first wife, Tamara, whom he believed had died in the Nazi horror, reappears. These three destinies, which are intertwined yet tear one another apart, are marked by fear. Yadwiga is terrified of the subway, the rumblings of the crowd, the ocean waves. When Tamara falls asleep, she sinks into an abyss and hears her dead children speaking to her. Masha is as mad as she is beautiful. Herman imagines repeatedly that the Nazis are in New York and that his food is served to him through a hole in the wall. Undermined by an unappeasable anguish, crushed by the web of complications life has spun around him, Herman lets himself be increasingly dominated by these women in whom he finds, respectively, the mother, the mistress, and the child. Shaken by events, unable to exercise his free will, lies be-come second nature to Herman. He betrays, tortures, and deceives the women. He is ruining their lives, and they know it. But in the end, they always return to him.

"I'm Herman, for good and for bad," Singer said repeatedly,[41] just as Flaubert used to say that he was Madame Bovary. It is tempting to draw parallels with *Enemies*. In Isaac's archives, there are records of many mysterious checks in the seventies made out to a woman named Dova Gerber, two hundred dollars on the twentieth of each month. What is behind this? Who is this woman? Why was Singer sending her money? According to Israel Zamir, Dova was a former mistress and a concentration camp survivor. Her passionate temperament inspired the character of Masha in *Enemies*.[42] Like Masha, Dova couldn't leave her mother and ended up going to live with her in Israel. When Singer, having promised to marry her, failed once again to keep his word, Dova threatened to take him to court. The monthly payments were made to avoid a trial. As in *Enemies*, Isaac's triangular love life was not without its complications. Israel Zamir relates what happened in the summer of 1975 when his father was invited to the Hebrew University in Jerusalem to receive an honorary doctorate.

> He traveled to Israel with Dova, and they stayed together at the Park Hotel in Tel Aviv. I remember the three of us were sitting and talking in his room when, unannounced, Alma suddenly appeared. My father blushed, and Dova turned pale.
>
> "Alma, what are you doing here?" he asked, fearful and annoyed.
>
> "I came for the ceremony," she answered calmly.
>
> I admired Alma's courage. She had decided that the affair with Dova had gone too far.[43]

Like Dvorah when told she wouldn't be going to Stockholm, Alma must have suffered as much as the heroines in *Enemies*. Thirty years later, Dvorah Telushkin refuses to elaborate upon the subject of Dova, a subject that still seems painful to her. But the strange thing is, these women's first instinct is always to protect Isaac, to take care of him, defend him, absolve him, and protect his reputation above all else, as if he were both their lover and their child, or as if he were the Magician of Lublin, "walking on a tightrope, two inches away from disaster . . . always on the edge of depression."[44] They knew that nothing had changed since his days of stealing from room to room and heart to heart. But they also knew that what might have passed for vaudeville was actually the tragic story of someone besieged on all sides in a world abandoned by God, a man who amazed and fascinated them because, more than anyone, he knew how to infuse life with enchantment.

TEN

"The Greatest Tragedy
Which Could Ever Happen to a Writer"

~

MAZEL TOV! Happy birthday! Dvorah's living room in New York echoed with joyful exclamations. A klezmer violinist charmed the guests sitting around Isaac in a circle. Alma stood by the door, watching the scene. It was 1984. Dvorah had a daughter, Rebecca; this party was a celebration of her fifth birthday and Isaac's eightieth. After bagels and lox, Singer blew out the candles in one powerful breath, then lowered his bald head as the guests clapped. But sometime later, he confided in Dvorah, "I am frightened. I have reached a situation vhere I cannot remember the names of my heroes. Vhen I sit down to write, it seems I am forgetting who is who. Deborah, this is the greatest tragedy vhich could ever happen to a writer."[1]

"FRESH LIKE A DAISY"

There had been no hint of impending tragedy. Between 1978 and 1984, Singer reaped the rewards of the Nobel Prize. More alert and dynamic than ever, he went wherever he was asked. In the fall of 1979, he lectured at the University of South Dakota and at Alfred University in upstate New York; he read stories at Grossinger's in the Catskills and spoke to students at St. Joseph's College in Brooklyn and at Kean College in New Jersey; he lectured at the Smithsonian Institution in Washington, D.C., at the University of Oregon in Eugene, at Coe College in Cedar Rapids, Iowa, stopped in Manhattan to give a speech at the Ninety-second Street Y, and then rushed to Minneapolis to see a performance of a play adapted from one of his short stories. Alma and Dvorah were concerned about his health. He wouldn't hear of it. "Aach!" he said. "I'm fresh like a daisy."[2]

As if this were not enough, in 1980, Isaac even took on a regular teaching position at the University of Miami. Of course he continued to write. He no longer typed himself, but every week he still sent his small notebook pages to the *Forward*; there an old-timer, Lewis Katz, was the only person able to decipher his handwritten manuscripts. Farrar, Straus and Giroux put out two new novels in English, *The Penitent* (1983) and *The King of the Fields* (1988), as well as two volumes of memoirs, *Lost in America* (1981) and *Love and Exile* (1984). Everyone close to Isaac was astonished at his energy and filled with admiration. He found it normal. "As long as the Almighty vill give me strength, I vant to vork," he kept repeating simply. "To make a few dollars. I vant to meet my readers."[3]

During this period there were also more and more adaptations of his works. Isaac was happy to collaborate. In 1979, *Teibele and Her Demon* was performed on Broadway. This wasn't his first work to be adapted to the stage—*Gimpel the Fool* and *The Mirror* had been performed in New York and at Yale in the sixties and seventies—but the *New York Post* claimed that the aura of the Nobel Prize contributed to the renaissance of the Jewish theater in New York. Three films were released as well: *The Magician of Lublin*, directed by Menahem Golan (1979), *Enemies*, directed by Paul Mazursky (1989), and above all, *Yentl*, directed by and starring Barbra Streisand in 1983. Singer's work even inspired an opera, *Gimpel the Fool*; the composer David Schiff explained that he wanted to go back to the melodies of klezmer music, traces of which can be found in Mahler, Stravinsky, and Kurt Weill.

At eighty, Singer was at the height of his fame. For some, he had become mythic. When he was invited to speak at the Sutton Place Synagogue in Manhattan in 1984, during the war in Lebanon, a limousine and four security guards were hired to protect him. He launched into a spirited defense of the Diaspora. "Judaism vas never as powerful as it is in the Diaspora," he said. "The struggle to survive in the Diaspora makes the Jew vork hard for his Jewishness."[4] As he got back inside the car, the crowd cheered him. The writer was becoming a symbol. But this did not go to his head or affect his daily life. Apart from his travels and lectures, he remained a Stakhanovite when it came to writing. "Let's work," he said to Dvorah. "An ox must work." He continued to fill his notebooks with amazing lists that show how his days were spent:

> 9–11: novel
> 11–12: wash, dress
> 12–2: walk, lunch
> 2–3: going to the F. [*Forward*]
> 3–6: write—4 times a week
> 6–6:30: [illegible]
> 7–8: supper (no overeat!)
> 8–11: people; movies; theater; reading
> Saturday: rest, reading[5]

AN ADMIRED OUTCAST

There was something otherworldly about this obstinate elderly man, impervious to new trends and fashions, who remained just as true to himself at eighty as at seventeen. This exasperated some people and fascinated others. Many Jewish intellectuals and journalists were relentless in their criticism. Under the title "Bashevis Singer, the Outcast," the French journal *L'Arche* openly vented its hostility. When *A Young Man in Search of Love* appeared in French in 1981, the journal published an astonishing indictment of the man it saw as the maverick of Yiddish letters.

> People familiar with the surviving milieu of Yiddish literature know that Bashevis Singer isn't much liked by his confreres, today's Yiddish writers . . . We were delighted that the high honor of the Nobel Prize was awarded to a hitherto unknown or little-known area of literature. But we certainly would have preferred the award go to some other representative of

that heritage and not to this writer who is outside the fold . . .

Is this literary intellectual, this leading figure in Yiddish literature, who successfully won an international audience by writing in Yiddish, and then acquired worldwide fame with his laurels, a Yiddishist? Well, actually, no, he is not. Yiddishism places great value—not to say glory—on the vernacular Jewish tongue and, more specifically, on its literature, considered as the modern pinnacle par excellence of Jewish culture.

However, Bashevis Singer attaches very little importance to the trio of founding-father patriarchs, i.e., Mendele Mocher Seforim, Sholem Aleichem, and Peretz, the true Abraham-Isaac-Jacob of Yiddishism, both emotionally and commemoratively. He owes virtually nothing to them, he doesn't fit in their tradition, doesn't draw on the same source of inspiration, neither praising nor berating the shtetl.[6]

Always the same criticism. Irreverence, betrayal of his own community, insistence on being his own, standing apart—Singer had already heard these reproaches in Warsaw at age thirty. He was criticized for daring to show Jews as ordinary people—or worse, as troublemakers. One day, in response to the question, "What is a Jew?" he answered, "The Jews are a people who can't sleep themselves and let nobody else sleep."[7]

Always the same criticism, but now even more virulent. Fifty years later, the Nobel Prize had added fuel to the fire, arousing feelings of envy and jealousy. Above all, history had left its mark. The Holocaust deepened the abyss that already separated Singer from some of his own people—especially from Orthodox Jews or Socialist Jews, who had no affection for him at all. In an interview with Agata Tuszynska, the painter Yonia Fajn, who met Singer on his eightieth birthday, explains:

If it hadn't been for the Holocaust, perhaps they would have had fewer reservations. But the mythology of the Holocaust, these last few years, requires that everyone die martyrs. Suddenly Singer arrives and says, they perished, that's true, but they were just ordinary people. How can such a thing be said

about people who are now a handful of ashes? Jews want legendary heroes, especially after so much pain and suffering.
After the complete destruction of their world, they needed
consolation . . . Literature had been their homeland for so many
years; they wanted it to serve as their calling card, so to speak,
and to provide what every homeland provides: a feeling of
pride, a feeling of security, identity, national character.[8]

This is at the heart of the paradox. There were people who felt
that the memorial constructed by Singer should be different—more
edifying and more solemn. But Isaac chose life—not idealized life, but
real life. His protagonists aren't heroes, they're Mr. and Mrs. Everyone. Yeshiva students and gossiping housewives, young women in
love and small-time crooks—none of these characters is particularly
illustrious. But from these tiny fragments of life, he extracted timeless
human truths. His Jewish hero wasn't the exemplar of one group but
a universal archetype, who could be appropriated by anyone and
whom everyone applauded. It was understandable that some people
felt betrayed. Others were captivated. In the eighties, the mainstream
newspapers made space for him in their columns, running many long
interviews and profiles. Isaac was more vocal than ever, on a variety of
topics.

On literature: "Man, more than all other animals, suffers from
boredom. Sometimes I think man's boredom begins in the womb . . .
There is no excuse for literature which does not entertain the reader,
or does not help the reader escape from the tedium of life."[9]

On style: "I think there should be a law that no book should be
larger than a thousand pages."[10]

On Yiddish: "I can't understand why Israel despises Yiddish, spits
on it. Yiddish is a language that accompanied the Jews to the ghettos,
the ovens, everywhere. Why don't Israelis study Yiddish in the Hebrew schools, the universities . . . ? Isn't Yiddish part of our culture?
Our fathers and our forefathers? Why be ashamed of them? With our
own hands, we educate our children against us!"[11]

On God: "I cannot believe in what the materialists say—that the
universe is a result of some explosion which took place billions of
years ago. If you don't believe that the universe is an accident, you

have to believe that there was some plan in its becoming—some de-
sign or some intelligence. And if you believe this, you already believe
in God. If you want to insist on calling Him nature, you can call Him
nature . . . You can call Him the absolute—it doesn't make any difference. The word 'God' is just as good as any other word."[12]

More God: "I'm inclined to believe that God and the world are
identical. God is everything: all spirit, all matter, what is, what was,
and what will be, as Spinoza conceived Him. However, according to
Spinoza, the Substance, with its infinite number of attributes, has no
will, no purpose. I don't believe in this part of Spinoza. I think that
we can just as well ascribe to the Substance will and designs and
purposes."[13]

On his "religion of protest": "I often say to myself that God *wants*
us to protest. He has had enough of those who praise Him all the time
and bless Him for all His cruelties to man and animals."[14]

On vegetarianism: "Vegetarianism is my religion, my protest. The
man who eats meat or the hunter agrees with the cruelties of Nature,
upholds with every bite of meat or fish that might is right."[15]

On the passions: "I have always felt that God was very frugal, very
stingy in bestowing gifts on us. He didn't give us enough intellect,
enough physical strength, but when He came to emotions, to passions,
He was very lavish. He gave us so many emotions and such strong
ones that every human being, even if he is an idiot, is a millionaire in
emotions."[16]

On literature again: "If Newton had really discovered gravitation
by seeing an apple fall and gravitation was valid for this particular apple only, Newton wouldn't have become famous. It was by generaliz-
ing the case . . . that gravitation became such an important discovery.
In literature it's the very opposite. If a real writer or painter wants
to describe or paint an apple, it has to be a unique apple. Because of
this, the moment the writer begins to dabble with generalizations
or with the masses, he's already out of his profession."[17]

And: "The most peculiar thing is that the more a person is unique,
the more he resembles others. That is the paradox of life."[18]

On autobiography: "In all my books I am there—my character is
there in one way or another. I haven't yet found a serious writer who
doesn't write about himself and his life."[19]

On politics: "I am actually conservative. I don't believe that by flattering the masses all the time we really achieve much."[20]

On his influences: "I was influenced more by Gogol than Sholem Aleichem . . . When I read [his] stories I said to myself, 'How is it possible that this man who lived a hundred years before me has stolen so many of my stories?' "[21]

On influencing others: "I don't think that I have influenced any author . . . If a writer is a writer he will always be himself, even if he has read a million books. And if he isn't . . . if he's an imitator, he will be an imitator even if he has read only a single book, because the imitation is in his character."[22]

On writers: "Writers can't change the world; we can't even make it worse."[23]

TERROR AND FURY

Not only do these thoughts show a man in full possession of his intellectual faculties, they are also quintessential Singer—someone both vulnerable and invincible, deliberately naïve at times, but always incredibly witty, quick, and subtle. It is therefore not hard to imagine Isaac's terror in confronting the first symptoms of Alzheimer's disease in 1984. Terror, as well as fury and rage. Loss of memory, the goal and driving force behind his work, shattered—how could he bear to see it happen? "My past is my future," he always said. Memory formed the very texture of his existence. It was his life, and vice versa. He foresaw the suffering that awaited him. He had a foreboding of the tragedy of the artist deprived of his creative faculty—the despair of a Beethoven going deaf or the distress of a Matisse gradually losing his sight.

Between 1984 and 1986, Isaac wasn't yet "officially" ill, but his personality changed imperceptibly. His character flaws became more pronounced. He became suspicious of everything and everyone. At times he was cruel, impulsive, and paranoid. He was subject to sudden mood changes. He was constantly afraid of not having enough money. He made Dvorah accompany him to the bank over and over again to verify that interest had been paid on his accounts. He kept telling anyone who would listen, "We're so poor. The publishers robbed us of everything."[24]

Other people's success, indeed life itself, became unendurable to him. It was as if he couldn't bear being unhappy alone. Already affected internally by the slowly advancing disease, he ruled his entourage with an iron hand. He was annoyed when Dvorah decided to learn Yiddish and give public performances. Would she be cutting into his sources of income? Was she a traitor, a viper he had nursed at his bosom? He cursed this young woman who had promised to take care of him until he died and was failing to live up to her promise. Dvorah was deeply distressed. How could he be so unjust, so egocentric? What had happened to their joyous laughter, their fulfilling work sessions, and their bonds of affection?

Twenty years later, in her Manhattan living room, sitting in front of a coffee table that had belonged to Isaac, Dvorah Telushkin doesn't hide the fact that she had made him promises early in their relationship: "I was young. I believed my promises. I assured him that I would take care of him all his life, even when he reached old age. I was sincere. I didn't realize, at twenty-two, what it meant to get old. It's like motherhood: No one can 'explain' it to you, you really only understand it with the birth of your first child."[25]

In 1986, Dvorah divorced Abraham Menashe; two years later, she married Rabbi Joseph Telushkin. Though it saddened her, she protected herself and, slowly, drifted apart from Isaac. He felt he was being abandoned. In her memoir, she shows him charming at one instant, odious and cutting the next, as he often was in this last period of his life. She also explains that she wrote the book in order to "make peace" with him. And when she takes you into her study to show you his hats and his typewriter, you realize without a doubt that she has found her peace. Her profound affection is intact.

REMISSIONS AND RELAPSES

There were long periods of remission between 1984 and 1986. The illness progressed stealthily. Usually, it was as though nothing had hap-

pened. Isaac would return to his old self. He would ask Dvorah to forgive him for his angry outbursts. He gave her birthday presents. They
shared rice pudding in a coffee shop and everything was exactly the
way it had been.

On July 4, 1986, America celebrated the hundredth anniversary of
the Statue of Liberty. Isaac and other celebrities were invited to Ellis
Island by Ed Koch, the mayor of New York. Afterward Singer said
that, throughout the ceremony, he recalled how, as a child in Poland,
he used to sit at his mother's feet while she read letters from America
to the people on Krochmalna Street who didn't know how to read.
How old was Isaac then? It doesn't matter. In any case, he didn't
know what the "statue" meant. But he understood that it was a welcome sight, something that involved salvation and freedom. So, in his
many imaginary trips to America, he had long conversations with the
statue—for she spoke Yiddish, of course! He also relived his arrival in
America a half century earlier, his extreme poverty, his tourist visa
that had to be renewed every six months, and his constant fear that he
would be deported and "see the statue for the last time."[26]

There were other good times in 1986, such as the visit of Yelena
Bonner, wife of Andrei Sakharov; she had cut Isaac's picture out of an
American magazine. He still had many projects. At eighty-two, with
Dvorah's help, Isaac was preparing an anthology of his early published writings from the *Forward*, he was getting ready to write a play
that he hoped would be a Broadway hit, he was thinking about a children's book on the history of philosophy, and he considered writing a
novel about the Jews in Khazar kingdom.

But every good moment had its dark underside. In 1986, in Wengen, Marie-Pierre Bay found him "lucid but tired, with absent moments." One day, he wandered straight down a mountain road. Some
hikers led him back to Alma, but his hand was bloodied, probably bit-
ten by a dog. On another occasion, in New York, he lost his temper
with Charles McGrath, Rachel McKenzie's successor at *The New
Yorker*, for rejecting one of his stories. Once, he seemed to be convers-
ing normally when he suddenly asked, "Have you had lunch with my
brother Joshua recently?" After that, he became lucid again and
plunged into infinite sadness. "I am completely *farblondzhet*," he said

in despair. He could be found lying on the couch, his blue eyes light and boyish, wide open, staring at the sky, terrified, as though he were praying. Or waiting for redemption.

LIKE A GHOST CUT OFF FROM EVERYTHING

In 1986, Alma decided they would move to Miami. "Your father has stopped writing because of the pain. I'm hoping that the warm weather will be good for him," she said to Israel Zamir when he came to see Isaac in New York shortly before their departure.[27] These were to be the last real exchanges between father and son. Israel showed Isaac a photo of Avihai, one of his grandsons. "That's me!" Isaac exclaimed on seeing his round face, ears sticking out, blue eyes, and light skin.[28] This was the first time he had shown any interest in his progeny. Several years earlier, when Israel had told him about the birth of his son, Isaac had said, "I'm glad about every baby you have. In my lectures I talk a lot about your children. America loves a writer with a big family. It makes for more closeness between the writer and his readers."[29]

Isaac looked at the Hebrew translation of *The Penitent*, which his son had brought for him from Israel. He began to read it, but his eyes slid from line to line. He thought the translation was bad and got angry. His son read it aloud and Isaac calmed down. He talked about Joseph Shapiro, the hero of the novel, and his desire to flee to Mea Shearim, the Orthodox neighborhood in Jerusalem, to get away from the ugliness, hypocrisy, and temptations of New York. He talked about modern man's feeling of alienation and that his penitence wasn't "a rebellion against the pleasures of life but a rebellion against despair." The return to religion was the only possible salvation.

Could Joseph Shapiro be Bashevis Singer? Could Isaac, in old age, have longed to return to the religious world of his youth, as some critics contend? Possibly. Dvorah recounts that in the last three years of his intellectual life she often caught him secretly reading the Yiddish weeklies written by religious groups in Brooklyn. But nothing was ever simple with Singer. To his son, Israel, who asked him this question, Isaac replied, "Nonsense. You know me. You also know that I have never been a saint and never will be."

That evening, after dinner, as Israel walked him back home, Isaac stopped to look at an attractive young woman. "I may be a bit deaf and blind and even a little senile, but I still notice a pretty face," he said to his son, with a charming smile. The temptation of Orthodoxy may haunt his protagonists, but Singer himself was no penitent.[30]

This was one of his last conversations. Everyone who saw him in Florida after that—Israel Zamir, Dvorah Telushkin, Roger and Dorothea Straus—experienced a similar shock. Isaac had become an old man, immobilized in a wheelchair, expressionless, with a blank stare. Two women bustled by his side, Alma and his nurse, Amparo Ruiz. They were both patient and devoted. Isaac didn't always recognize them. He was cut off, self-absorbed, exiled once again from his surroundings. Where was he? In which inaccessible place? When he awoke from his torpor, he asked for his brother Joshua. Or he began to search feverishly for his passport and other documents. He was always polite and called his nurse "darling." One day, in a semicomatose state, he shouted, "Naamah!" the name of the demon who appeared in the 969-year-old Methuselah's dream and united herself with him one last time just before his death.[31]

One of his last pronouncements was for Alma: "I wasn't a good husband to you." After several cerebral hemorrhages and a stay in the hospital—he had been diagnosed with colon cancer—Isaac was transferred to a nursing home. It was there that, on a Wednesday, at about 4:00 p.m., he opened his blue eyes for the last time—opened them wide, seemed to stare up at the sky, then closed them quietly.[32]

The Florida death certificate reads as follows:

Isaac Bashevis Singer, sex male
Date of death: July 24, 1991, age 87
Date of birth: July 14, 1904, place: Poland
Place of death: Nursing home
Son of Pinchos Synger and Basheve Silverman
Cause:

       cardio-respiratory arrest   6 months

cancer of colon   1 year
organic brain syndrome   1 year

"THE WORLD IS FULL OF POWERS THAT WE DON'T KNOW"[33]

Singer didn't really believe in death. He thought that souls returned to hover among the living in another guise. "As far as God is concerned, it doesn't make sense for Him to send a soul into the world only once," he used to joke.[34] He had convinced himself that he had already lived through several previous incarnations. He believed in ghosts, spirits, demons, imps. On the day of his funeral, these demons had a field day. When the rabbi started to speak, the microphone began squeaking and gurgling, and it was impossible to hear what he was saying. Singer's son had wanted his father buried in Israel, but Alma had been against it. She preferred—perhaps for financial reasons?—that Isaac be buried at the Beth-El cemetery in New Jersey, a few yards from her first husband. There was a misprint on his tombstone. The engraving said "Noble" instead of "Nobel," as if the mischievous aristocrat of Yiddish letters was still trying to send messages from beyond the grave.[35]

Alma remained haunted by the look in his eyes at the end. His wide-open gaze seemed to beg for help, but she was powerless. She had sacrificed everything for Isaac. She had given up a comfortable existence to run away with a penniless, unknown Yiddish writer, and resigned herself to hardly seeing her children. Her daughter Inge, who died a year before Isaac, openly reproached her for abandoning the family. She had worked tirelessly, for herself and her husband, had put up with his escapades, and had always been considered insignificant next to him. Yet after his death, she said to Dvorah, "My life was always him, his work. I had nothing else . . . You know, when the doctors told me there was no hope . . . I told them, 'I don't care. No matter what, I want him alive.' . . . I wanted him any way that I could have him."[36]

In October 1993, the two women worked alone in what was once the "chaos room." They were clearing out Isaac's papers, an enormous

task. There were entire boxes filled with letters, including those from
his old Warsaw friend Aaron Zeitlin, and other enthusiastically admiring ones from Henry Miller and countless unknowns. There were
boxes of old newspapers and manuscripts, which Isaac had believed
lost or irreparably damaged by a flood. There were notebooks, photos,
unpublished works. All of this was supposed to go by prearrangement
to the Harry Ransom Center at the University of Texas at Austin,
where the Singer archive took its place next to those of Saul Bellow,
Phillip Roth, Gertrude Stein, and Albert Einstein. Alma sighed,
"Now, even this room is empty."[37]

Ten years later, in Austin, the cataloging is still not complete. The
woman in charge of the collection apologizes, "If you had seen what
state all this was in when we received it . . . papers accumulated for
over fifty years, piled up chaotically, loose sheets all mixed up together.
It took us an incredible amount of time to sort through these things."
Singer's personal effects are kept a short distance away, at the Undergraduate Library. To see them, it is necessary to make an appointment
and you must wear gloves. "It's exhilarating, isn't it? Everyone gets
very excited when they come into this room," says the woman who
opens the door. It would be more appropriate to say pathetic or absurd. The collection is made up of a strange assortment of odds and
ends, including thick horn-rimmed glasses; a brown leather Eterna
wristwatch; a salmon-colored satin yarmulke; an authentic Borsalino
hat, monogrammed inside with three small initials, IBS; and even a
pair of Alma's stockings. But there are also countless medals, plaques,
awards—the National Book Award medal, medals from Brandeis
University, the Buber Rosenzweig medal, the S. Y. Agnon Gold
Medal, awards from the Decalogue Society of Chicago Lawyers, from
the National Institute of Arts and Letters, the Shirley Kravitz Children's Book Award, the small plaque from the National Conference
of Christians and Jews, and many more, including the Nobel Prize
medal with the bearded profile of Alfred Nobel on one side and a classical scene with a muse playing the cittern on the other. Last but not
least, there is a big black metal Underwood with Hebrew letters and a
carriage that moves right to left. One of his typewriters? Not according to Singer. It was a living being, an extension of his fingers, a metal

box inhabited by a highly discriminating spirit, who would suddenly stop working when he disagreed with a word or expression. Isaac had typed many still unpublished works on that machine, including an autobiography, *Di Mishpokhe* (The Family), and at least five novels: *Der Zindiker Meskiekh* (The Sinful Messiah); *Der Man fun Khaloymes* (The Man of Dreams); *Der Fartribener Zun* (The Exiled Son), which recalls *The Certificate*; *Der Weg Aheim* (The Way Home); and a gangster novel, *Yarme un Keyle* (Yarme and Keyle), populated with con men, blackmailers, murderers, and prostitutes in a Poland that was still a part of the czarist empire.[38]

Why haven't these works been published? In some cases, Isaac was dissatisfied with what he had written; he preferred that the writings remain in Yiddish and that no one "translate them after his death." Alluding to Kafka, he used to say, "There is no Max Brod in my life. I hope my heirs will respect this wish. I cannot *burn* my manuscripts. They are published."[39]

Isaac's notebooks are in Austin, also. There are eighty-four in all, from different periods, in a variety of colors, sizes, and brands. There are drawings of birds, profiles, boots, and caricatures, all of which show the extent to which Isaac "saw" his protagonists. There are jottings of different tentative titles—for *The Spinoza of Market Street*, for example: "The Spinoza of Krochmalna Street," "Blessed Spinoza," "Under the Aspect of Eternity," or "Spinoza on Market Street." There are lists of numbers like the one dated November 1984: "*Times* 50; Harvard 2,268; Univ. Miami 2,567.02, National Committee for literary arts 115; Campbell Soup 57.50; Yivo 1,000." Then there is also the occasional telephone number, Dvorah's or his own, already written in shaky handwriting. Elsewhere, there is a poem written in English, penned in his small, refined, intelligent handwriting. It isn't dated, but its tone is one of disillusionment:

> *So much wisdom so much advice*
> *so much knowledge in my sack . . .*
> *it almost breaks my heart*

And farther down—are these words of self-criticism?

He has lost the meaning
missed the hint
misinterpreted, misunderstood
done too little or too much.

We also find the kinds of lists Isaac was so fond of, like the one classifying his favorite readings:

1. The Bible
2. *The Best of Pearls* by Moses Hayyim Luzzatto
3. *Crime and Punishment*
4. *Anna Karenina*
5. Gogol's short stories
6. *Madame Bovary*
7. E. A. Poe
8. *Pan* by Knut Hamsun
9. Swedenborg, *Heaven and Hell*
10. *The Phantasmas of the Living*

In the midst of all these treasures, we find Isaac's will, or rather wills. There are many successive versions, codicils, and revisions. Singer, so fearful of poverty, died with an estimated fortune of three million dollars, which he left entirely to Alma. She didn't survive him for long: she died four and a half years later, on January 11, 1996.

"A DOT IN GOD'S INFINITE BOOK"

Manhattan, 2002. In the offices of the *Forward*, there are no traces of Singer. Not a single photograph or portrait. "It's true, he lent prestige to the paper, but feelings about him were mixed," explains Kobi Weitzner, a journalist at the *Forward* and one of the last playwrights to still write in Yiddish. "For the old-timers, he was never really integrated into the editorial staff. He was right-wing, whereas everyone here was left-wing. He was misanthropic, distrusted humanity, and even in his writing, he went his separate way. He was a free electron.

People were wary of him as someone slightly disturbing." Success hardly helped matters. "Jews are not forgiven for their failures. Nor are they forgiven for their successes," jests Weitzner. "By the way, do you know why Jesus isn't the son of God? Because no Jew could accept the idea that another Jew is the son of God."[40]

Manhattan, 2002. "Isaac Singer, an American writer?" wonders Dorothea Straus. "No, he was fundamentally European. He lived here, that's all. He spoke in libraries, gave readings, and went on lecture tours. But all his writings were about Jews of European descent living in the United States. He stuck to places he knew. He hated the East Side [of New York] because there were no cafeterias."[41]

Leoncin, 2001. Here, too, apparently, Isaac is not a native son. Far from it. There is no trace of his childhood home or even of Jewish life of the past, except for the sign indicating Isaac Bashevis Singer Street, with its anti-Semitic graffiti. "There was once a mayor who dreamed of restoring the town's Jewish past, of building a cultural center, a memorial room, and similar things. But the residents didn't like him," writes Agata Tuszynska. "He was defeated in the elections . . . He succeeded only in naming a Leoncin street after his eminent compatriot . . . But no one wanted to live on Isaac Bashevis Singer Street. So the road to the school was chosen by private agreement. It has no residential housing, so none of the Leoncin inhabitants are forced to have a Jewish address they don't want."[42]

Neither Jewish nor American nor Polish. Singer knew he was an exile everywhere and would always remain so. He didn't belong to any single geographical location. Nor did he belong in the present or the past—a past that no longer existed. He was, as he put it, "lost in the world."[43] He was resigned to this fact and exploited it. He saw himself as "a letter or a dot in God's infinite book." But, he said, "Even if I am an error in God's work, I can't be completely erased." For "God is the sum total not only of all deeds but also of all the possibilities."[44]

Notes

PREFACE

1. Isaac Bashevis Singer and Richard Burgin, *Conversations with Isaac Bashevis Singer* (Garden City, NY: Doubleday, 1985), pp. 35–37.

ONE. *"A STRONGHOLD OF JEWISH PURITANISM"*

1. Isaac Bashevis Singer, *In My Father's Court*, trans. Channah Kleinerman-Goldstein, Elaine Gottlieb, and Joseph Singer (New York: Farrar, Straus and Giroux, 1966), p. 77.
2. Daniel Tollet, *Histoire des Juifs en Pologne du XVIe siècle à nos jours* (Paris: Presses Universitaires de France, 1992), p. 301.
3. Author's interview with Marie-Pierre Bay, Paris, October 12, 2000. Regarding his birthplace, in "One Day of Happiness," Singer writes that he was born in Radzymin and not Leoncin. He subsequently said he had wanted to simplify matters after Radzymin was listed as his official birthplace on his birth certificate through an error at the registry. The anecdote is significant. It demonstrates how important it is to be circumspect in considering the autobiographical part of his work, which Singer, by the way, clearly stated was autobiographical fiction.
4. Agata Tuszynska, *Singer, paysages de la mémoire*, trans. Jean-Yves Erhel (Paris: Noir sur Blanc, 2002), p. 385. [The English version of this book, *Lost Landscapes: In Search of Isaac Bashevis Singer and the Jews of Poland*, trans. Madeline G. Levine (New York: William Morrow, 1998), seems to differ from the French version. I could not find this quote in the English translation.—Trans.]
5. I. J. Singer, *Of a World That Is No More* (New York: Vanguard Press, 1970). The original Yiddish title is *Fun a velt vos iz nishto mer* (New York: Farlag Mantones, 1946).
6. Esther Kreitman, *The Dance of Demons* (Poland: Brzoza, 1936). The English version is *Deborah*, trans. Maurice Carr (New York: St. Martin's Press, 1983).
7. Tollet, *Histoire des Juifs*, preface by Pierre Chanu, p. 8.
8. Singer, *In My Father's Court*, p. 49. Singer said he had used his maternal grandfather

as the model for the character of Rabbi Benish in his first novel, *Shoten an Goray* (*Satan in Goray*).

9. Ibid., pp. 67–68.

10. Ibid.

11. Singer and Burgin, *Conversations*, p. 81.

12. Ibid., pp. 11, 12.

13. Ibid., pp. 12–13.

14. Singer, *In My Father's Court*, pp. 63–64.

15. Ibid., p. 37.

16. I. J. Singer, *Of a World That Is No More*, pp. 29–30.

17. Singer, *In My Father's Court*, p. 53.

18. Guerchon Hel and Nathanel Gryn, *Memory Book of the Jewish Community of Radzymin* (Tel Aviv: Encyclopédie de la diaspora, 1975). My special thanks to Paul Morgensztern, a native of Radzymin who lived in the town until 1939, for lending me this memory book.

19. Singer, *In My Father's Court*, p. 56.

20. Ibid., p. 58.

TWO. "THE GOLD MINE OF KROCHMALNA STREET"

1. Singer and Burgin, *Conversations*, p. 14.

2. Ibid., pp. 9–10. Singer adds that he also writes about things that take place in America, but that even in the American part of his work, Poland is omnipresent and just beneath the surface. It is easier and more natural for him to "go back to these years in Warsaw than to any other time."

3. *Krochmal* means "starch" in Polish. According to the newspaper *Gazeta Wyborcza*, the street got its name from a starch and dye factory that existed there until 1847.

4. Author's interview with Agata Tuszynska and *Lost Landscapes*, p. 10.

5. Singer, *In My Father's Court*, p. 226.

6. Author's conversation with Szulim Rozenberg, Paris, September 14 and October 5, 2000.

7. Singer, *In My Father's Court*, p. 70.

8. Joel Blocker and Richard Eldman, "An Interview with Isaac Bashevis Singer," *Commentary*, November 1963, pp. 364–72. Reprinted in Grace Farrell, ed., *Isaac Bashevis Singer: Conversations* (Jackson: University Press of Mississippi, 1992), p. 11.

9. Isaac Bashevis Singer, *More Stories from My Father's Court*, trans. Curt Leviant (New York: Farrar, Straus and Giroux, 2000), p. 159.

10. Éveline Thévenard-Cahn, "Autobiographies," *L'Arc*, no. 93.

11. Singer, *In My Father's Court*, p. 11.

12. Ibid., pp. 15–16.

13. Singer's father and mother belonged to two separate currents of Judaism of the period. Pinchos Menahem belonged to the Hasidim (the "pious"), the disciples of Baal Shem Tov; Bathsheba to the Mitnagdim (the "opponents"), who did not accept this mystical, popular current. The division between Hasidim and Mitnagdim was extreme.

14. Isaac Bashevis Singer and Ira Moskowitz, *A Little Boy in Search of God: Mysticism in a Personal Light* (Garden City, NY: Doubleday, 1976), p. 36.

15. Singer and Burgin, *Conversations*, p. 107.
16. Let us note in passing that in doing this Singer was not inventing anything. He was drawing on an ancient tradition of Polish-Jewish folklore and literature. For the contribution of traditional Yiddish literature in Singer's work, see Henri Lewi, *Isaac Bashevis Singer: La génération du déluge* (Paris: Le Cerf, 2001). On the supernatural in Singer's work, see Pierre Chartier, "Le Surnaturel: Du dibbouk au don Juan," *L'Arc*, no. 93. See also Éveline Thévenard-Cahn's dissertation, "Dualité et tension dans l'oeuvre de I. B. Singer" (Paris: Université de Paris-VII, 1983).
17. Singer and Moskowitz, *A Little Boy in Search of God*, p. 15.
18. Ibid., p. 57.
19. Ibid., p. 45.
20. Blocker and Eldman, "Interview with Isaac Bashevis Singer," in Farrell, *Isaac Bashevis Singer*, p. 12.
21. Singer and Moskowitz, *A Little Boy in Search of God*, p. 47.
22. Ibid., p. 59.
23. Ibid., p. 61.
24. Ibid., p. 93.
25. Ibid., p. 87.
26. Ibid., p. 88.
27. Singer, *In My Father's Court*, p. 78.
28. *L'Illustration, années 1917–1919* (Paris: Le Livre de Paris), p. 55.
29. Singer and Moskowitz, *A Little Boy in Search of God*, pp. 93–95.

THREE. A "PRIVATE WAR AGAINST THE ALMIGHTY"

1. Singer, *In My Father's Court*, p. 268.
2. Singer, *More Stories from My Father's Court*, p. 92.
3. Thévenard-Cahn, "Autobiographies," p. 14.
4. Singer, *In My Father's Court*, p. 268.
5. Ibid., p. 51.
6. Ibid., pp. 268–69.
7. Ibid., p. 270.
8. Ibid., p. 272.
9. Ibid., pp. 273–74.
10. Ibid., p. 287.
11. Ibid., p. 291.
12. Singer and Moskowitz, *A Little Boy in Search of God*, pp. 99–109, 131.
13. Ibid., pp. 105, 109.
14. Ibid., p. 117.
15. *Anthony Burgess et Isaac Bashevis Singer, Recontre au sommet* (Paris: Mille et Une Nuits-Arte éditions, 1998). This dialogue is the transcript of an interview aired on Swedish television in 1985. The transcript and commentary are by Isy Morgansztern, for whom this meeting was "something of an unofficial summit between Jews and Catholics." Singer said something similar to his son, Israel Zamir: "He knew that Satan does the work of the Holy-One-Blessed-Be-He." Israel Zamir, *Journey to My Father, Isaac Bashevis Singer*, trans. Barbara Harshav (New York: Arcade Publishing, 1995), p. 210.

16. Singer and Burgin, *Conversations*, p. 116.

17. Singer, *In My Father's Court*, p. 297.

18. Ibid., p. 304.

19. Ibid., p. 305.

20. Ibid., p. 307.

21. Ibid., pp. 239–40.

22. Ibid., pp. 294–95.

23. Ibid., p. 240.

24. Singer and Moskowitz, *A Little Boy in Search of God*, pp. 123, 125.

25. Author's conversation with Lydie Lachenal, Paris, January 12, 2001. Only two issues of the journal were published. These were reprinted in one volume titled *"Khaliastra La Bande," revue littéraire, Varsovie 1922–Paris 1924* (Paris: Lachenal et Ritter, 1989). It was edited by Rachel Ertel, translated from the Yiddish and annotated by Charles Dobzynski, Jacques Mandelbaum, and Bernard Vaisbrot, and from the Italian by Jean-Baptiste Para, and includes Rachel Ertel's essay *"Khaliastra* et la modernité européenne" as well as a text by Israel Joshua Singer, "Sans l'obscurité," translated by Jacques Mandelbaum.

26. Singer, *In My Father's Court*, p. 305.

27. Isaac Bashevis Singer, *A Young Man in Search of Love* (Garden City, NY: Doubleday, 1978), p. 161.

FOUR. "THE SERVANT OF TWO IDOLS"

1. Samuel Schneiderman interviewed by Paul Kresh in *Isaac Bashevis Singer: The Magician of West 86th Street* (New York: Dial Press, 1979), pp. 88–89. Indeed, Singer had few close friends, except for the memoir writer J. J. Trunk, twenty years his senior, and Aaron Zeitlin, a poet whom Isaac regarded as a master. In 1932, Singer and Zeitlin founded *Globus*, a short-lived literary magazine. In 1934, *Globus* published the serialized installments of Isaac's first novel, *Shoten an Goray* (*Satan in Goray*). When the Yiddish section of the Warsaw PEN Club decided to publish this work as a book, Zeitlin wrote the introduction.

2. Singer, *A Young Man in Search of Love*, p. 34.

3. Singer and Moskowitz, *A Little Boy in Search of God*, pp. 142–43.

4. Author's conversation with Marie-Pierre Bay.

5. Author's conversation with Szulim Rozenberg.

6. Ibid.

7. Author's conversation with Michal Friedman, Warsaw, July 30, 2001.

8. Isaac Bashevis Singer, *Lost in America* (Garden City, NY: Doubleday, 1981), p. 6.

9. Singer, *A Young Man in Search of Love*, p. 44.

10. See the article by Marc Saporta in *L'Arc*, no. 93, p. 46.

11. Lester Goran, *The Bright Streets of Surfside: The Memoir of a Friendship with Isaac Bashevis Singer* (Kent, OH: Kent State University Press, 1994), p. 11.

12. Singer, *A Young Man in Search of Love*, p. 36.

13. Ibid., p. 34.

14. Isaac Bashevis Singer, *The Certificate*, trans. Leonard Wolf (New York: Farrar, Straus and Giroux, 1992), p. 169.

15. Singer and Moskowitz, *A Little Boy in Search of God*, p. 199.

16. Singer, *A Young Man in Search of Love*, pp. 108–109.

17. Ibid., p. 109.

18. This story, never translated, inspired the short story "Two Corpses Go Dancing," written in 1943.

19. Singer, *A Young Man in Search of Love*, p. 112.

20. Singer, *The Certificate*, p. 222.

21. Singer, *A Young Man in Search of Love*, p. 91.

22. Singer, *Lost in America*, p. 1.

23. Ibid., p. 3.

24. Ibid., p. 1.

25. Singer, *A Young Man in Search of Love*, pp. 149, 147.

26. Ibid., p. 176.

27. Ibid., p. 66.

28. Singer, *Lost in America*, p. 14. According to Israel Zamir, Isaac and Runya were married in a civil ceremony in Poland.

29. Singer, *A Young Man in Search of Love*, p. 98.

30. Ibid., p. 177.

31. Lewi, *Isaac Bashevis Singer*, p. 41.

FIVE. "A BARE SOUL"

1. Singer, *Lost in America*, p. 54.

2. Ibid., p. 4.

3. Author's conversation with Israel Zamir, Paris, June 28, 2002.

4. Nancy Green, *L'Odyssée des Émigrants* (Paris: Gallimard, 1994), p. 32.

5. Zamir, *Journey to My Father*, pp. 17–18.

6. Isaac Bashevis Singer, *Collected Stories: "A Friend of Kafka" to "Passions"* (New York: Library of America, 2004), p. 210.

7. *L'Illustration*, Spring 1935.

8. "All the snobs of Europe strove to be aboard . . . I declined the privilege . . . I feared an imminent Hitler invasion." Singer, *Lost in America*, p. 63.

9. Ibid., pp. 73–74.

10. Ibid., p. 76.

11. Henry Roth, *Call It Sleep* (New York: Cooper Square Publishers, 1976), pp. 3–4.

12. Green, *L'Odyssée des Émigrants*, p. 68.

13. Author's conversation with Rachel Ertel, Paris, October 18, 2001.

14. Rachel Ertel, *Le Roman Juif Américain: Une Écriteur Minoritaire* (Paris: Payot, 1980), pp. 57–59.

15. Roth, *Call It Sleep*, pp. 5–6.

16. Singer, *Lost in America*, p. 113.

17. Ibid., p. 106.

18. *Isaac in America*, film by Avram Nowk, 1994.

19. Singer, *Lost in America*, p. 107.

20. Kresh, *Isaac Bashevis Singer*, p. 146.

21. Singer, *Lost in America*, p. 120.

22. Ibid., p. 121.

23. Ibid., p. 199.

24. Janet Hadda, *Isaac Bashevis Singer: A Life* (New York: Oxford University Press, 1997), p. 96.

25. Ibid., pp. 97–98.

26. Ibid., pp. 93–108.

27. Author's interview with Marie-Pierre Bay, Paris, October 12, 2000.

28. *L'Illustration*, December 1939–January 1940.

SIX. "THE LANGUAGE OF NO ONE"

1. *Newsweek*, August 1942; *New York Times*, November 25 and 26, 1942.

2. Raul Hilberg, *The Destruction of the European Jews* (New York: Holmes & Meier, 1985), p. 312.

3. Singer, *Lost in America*, p. 247.

4. See Laurence Anter, "Hommage à Joshua," *L'Arc*, no. 93.

5. Singer and Burgin, *Conversations*, p. 166.

6. Singer, *Lost in America*, p. 120.

7. *Shoten an Goray un Anderer Dertailungen* (New York: Farlag Mantones, 1943). Singer's novel *Der Zindiker Meshiekh* (The Fisherman Messiah) also appeared in the *Forward*, but because Singer wasn't entirely pleased with it, this novel, along with *Der Man Fun Khaloymes* (The Man of Dreams), was never translated.

8. Isaac Bashevis Singer, *The Family Moskat*, trans. A. H. Gross (New York: Alfred A. Knopf, 1950), p. 26.

9. Singer and Burgin, *Conversations*, p. 26.

10. Pierre Dommergues, *Le Monde*, October 9, 1970.

11. Singer and Burgin, *Conversations*, p. 19.

12. Ibid., p. 62.

13. Interview with Rachel Ertel conducted by Marion Van Renterghem, *Le Monde des Livres*, May 3, 1997.

14. Singer and Burgin, *Conversations*, p. 70.

15. Isaac Bashevis Singer, "On Translating My Books," *The World of Translation* (New York: PEN American Center, 1971), pp. 109–11. [Similar passages can be found in Isaac Bashevis Singer, "Why Shouldn't I Write in Yiddish?" quoted in Dvorah Telushkin, *Master of Dreams: A Memoir of Isaac Bashevis Singer* (New York: William Morrow, 1997), p. 226, and in an excerpt of a speech quoted in Zamir, *Journey to My Father*, p. 170: "How many words does English have for 'poor'? Maybe half a dozen at most. But in Yiddish we've got pauper, beggar, destitute, wretched, shlepper, good-for-nothing, owner of a cabbage head, shirtless, miserable pauper, deep in grief, chopped grief, and just everyday grief. You can say that a man swallows his saliva, that he forgot the shape of a coin, that he drops dead from hunger three times a day, that things go as bad for him as for a wicked person in the next world or a saint in this world, that he carries his soul on the end of his nose. You can say that he stumbles like a fool, that he barely has enough for water and grits, that all year long is Passover for him, since he doesn't see a slice of bread. You can even call him Rothschild, with a slight wink, and everyone will understand that he's dying of hunger. Only a crazy person would trade such a rich language for English."—trans.]

16. Author's conversation with Rachel Ertel.

17. Singer and Burgin, *Conversations*, p. 73.

18. Ibid., p. 61.

SEVEN. THE CONQUEST OF AMERICA

1. This is the subtitle of Paul Kresh's biography, *Isaac Bashevis Singer: The Magician of West 86th Street*.
2. Quoted ibid., pp. 233, 364.
3. Author's telephone conversation with Robert Giroux, New York, May 2, 2002.
4. Hadda, *Isaac Bashevis Singer*, p. 131.
5. Author's conversation with Delphine Bechtel, Paris, June 28, 2001.
6. D. Roskies, "IBS un zayne sheydim," *De goldene keyt*, no. 134, 1992.
7. Henri Lewi, "Pourquoi IBS ne voulait pas être traduit du texte Yiddish" ("Why IBS did not want to be translated from the Yiddish"), unpublished article.
8. Unpublished translation from the Yiddish by Batia Baum.
9. Isaac Bashevis Singer, "The Mirror," trans. Norbert Guterman, in *Gimpel the Fool and Other Stories* (New York: Farrar, Straus and Giroux, 1978), pp. 87–88.
10. See Khoné Shmeruk, "IBS af di shpurn fun zayn oytobiografye," *Di goldene keyt*, no. 115, 1985, as well as Lewi, "Pourquoi IBS ne voulait pas être traduit."
11. Pierre Lepape, "Le dictionnaire intime de Milan Kundera," *Le Monde*, July 4, 2001.
12. Lewi, "Pourquoi IBS ne voulait pas être traduit."
13. See Lewi, *Isaac Bashevis Singer*.
14. Author's conversation with Henri Lewi, June 12, 2001.
15. Author's conversation with Delphine Bechtel.
16. Khoné Shmeruk, "Lettre à la rédaction," *Di goldene keyt*, no. 134, 1992.
17. "La traduction de l'oeuvre d'Isaac Bashevis Singer" ("Translation of Isaac Bashevis Singer's Work"), roundtable with Seth Wolitz and Henri Lewi, Bibliothèque Medem, June 1, 2002. This roundtable was part of a series of lectures titled "Les Mondes d'Isaac Bashevis Singer," from January 23 to June 12, 2002.
18. Singer, "On Translating My Books," p. 111.
19. Quoted by Herbert R. Lottman in "I. B. Singer, Storyteller," *New York Times Book Review*, June 25, 1972, p. 5; reprinted in Farrell, *Isaac Bashevis Singer*, pp. 116–17.
20. Zamir, *Journey to My Father*, pp. 43–44.
21. Ibid., p. 22.
22. Singer and Burgin, *Conversations*, pp. 21–22.
23. Author's conversation with Marie-Pierre Bay.
24. Zamir, *Journey to My Father*, p. 92.
25. Author's conversation with Marie-Pierre Bay.
26. Author's conversation with Dorothea Straus, New York, April 30, 2002.
27. Singer, "On Translating My Books," p. 113.
28. Author's conversation with Dorothea Straus.
29. Ibid.; see also Kresh, *Isaac Bashevis Singer*, pp. 226–28.
30. Author's conversation with Dorothea Straus.
31. Zamir, *Journey to My Father*, p. 93.
32. Ibid.
33. Ibid.

EIGHT. SINGER VERSUS SINGER

1. Isaac Bashevis Singer, "What It Takes to Be a Jewish Writer," *National Jewish Monthly*, November 1963.
2. Singer and Burgin, *Conversations*, p. 133.

3. Farrell, *Isaac Bashevis Singer*, p. 118.
4. Telushkin, *Master of Dreams*, p. 95.
5. Singer and Burgin, *Conversations*, p. 146.
6. Farrell, *Isaac Bashevis Singer*, p. 118.
7. Telushkin, *Master of Dreams*, p. 94.
8. Letter from Mrs. Josephine Bayne, New York, in Singer Archives, Harry Ransom Center, University of Texas at Austin.
9. Kresh, *Isaac Bashevis Singer*, pp. 199, 281.
10. Letter from Elaine Gottlieb, May 6, 1996, Singer Archives.
11. Robert Giroux quoted in Ilan Stavans, ed., *Isaac Bashevis Singer: An Album* (New York: Library of America, 2004), p. 107.
12. Author's conversation with Herbert Lottman, Paris, February 10, 2003.
13. Author's conversation with André Bay, La Frette, January 11, 2002.
14. Letter in German from Claudio Magris, September 18, 1966, Singer Archives.
15. Telushkin, *Master of Dreams*, p. 177.
16. Zamir, *Journey to My Father*, pp. 177–78.
17. André Bay, *L'Arc*, no. 93, p. 111.
18. Quoted in Kresh, *Isaac Bashevis Singer*, pp. 335, 367.
19. Michael Mohrt, "Le Dibbouk et les cosmonauts," *L'Air du large: Essais sur le roman étranger* (Paris: Gallimard, 1970), pp. 270–80.
20. Cynthia Ozick, "Envy; or, Yiddish in America," in *The Pagan Rabbi* (New York: Alfred A. Knopf, 1971), pp. 46–48.
21. Irving Howe, "Demonic Fiction of a Yiddish Modernist," *Commentary* 30 (October 1960): 350–53; quoted in Kresh, *Isaac Bashevis Singer*, p. 117.
22. Telushkin, *Master of Dreams*, p. 3.
23. Letter from Maurice Carr, January 14, 1952, Singer Archives.
24. Letter from Maurice Carr, January 20, 1967, ibid.
25. Letter from Maurice Carr, July 28, 1954, ibid.
26. Zamir, *Journey to My Father*, p. 10.
27. Ibid., p. 103.
28. Ibid., pp. 10, 237.
29. Ibid., p. 99.
30. Ibid., pp. 14–15.
31. Isaac Bashevis Singer, "The Son," in *Collected Stories*, pp. 309, 212–13.
32. Author's conversation with Israel Zamir, Paris, June 28, 2002.
33. Author's conversation with Israel Zamir, Paris, June 29, 2002; see also Zamir, *Journey to My Father*, p. 23.
34. Author's conversation with Israel Zamir, June 28, 2002.
35. Letter dated 1974, Singer Archives.

NINE. *"HOW LONG CAN A MAN BE SURPRISED? HOW LONG CAN A MAN BE HAPPY?"*

1. Telushkin, *Master of Dreams*, pp. 181, 182.
2. Ibid., pp. 151, 37, 39.
3. Ibid., p. 19.
4. Ibid., pp. 16–17. (The letter is in the Singer Archives. It includes her address and tele-

phone number. At Dvorah Menashe Telushkin's request, her correspondence with Singer has been removed from the archives, except for this very first letter, dated August 29, 1975.)

5. Ibid., pp. 21–22.
6. Ibid., p. 69.
7. Ibid., p. 45.
8. Author's interview with Dvorah Telushkin, New York, July 30, 2002.
9. Ibid.
10. Ibid.
11. Author's interview with Marie-Pierre Bay.
12. Telushkin, *Master of Dreams*, p. 136.
13. "It contained all kinds of things," says Roger Straus. "Short stories, essays, personal and professional letters . . . His study was in real shambles. Singer was afraid that these papers would be destroyed or used without his permission." Author's conversation with Roger Straus, New York, May 1, 2002.
14. Telushkin, *Master of Dreams*, p. 182.
15. The address is Surfside Towers, #703, Collins Avenue, Miami Beach. A letter from the attorney David J. Mandel, dated March 26, 1973, says that the apartment was acquired for fifty-four thousand dollars, which confirms that, starting in the early seventies, the Singers were sufficiently well off financially for Isaac, who was so loath to spend money, to agree to this investment.
16. Letter from Alma Singer to Herbert and Michèle Lottman, October 14, 1978, Herbert Lottman Archives, Paris.
17. Article by Jean-Louis Ezine, *Les Nouvelles littéraires*, October 12, 1978.
18. Zamir, *Journey to My Father*, pp. 142, 144.
19. Knut Ahnlund's books include *Isaac B. Singer, Hans Sprak och Hans Värld* (Isaac B. Singer, His Language and His World) (Stockholm: Brombergs, 1978).
20. Author's interview with Knut Ahnlund, Stockholm, September 19, 2001.
21. Telushkin, *Master of Dreams*, p. 175.
22. Quoted in Kresh, *Isaac Bashevis Singer*, p. 398.
23. Quoted in Hadda, *Isaac Bashevis Singer*, p. 173.
24. Quoted in ibid., pp. 172–74.
25. Telushkin, *Master of Dreams*, p. 184.
26. Ibid., p. 193.
27. Author's interview with Dorotea Bromberg, Stockholm, September 18, 2001.
28. Dorothea Straus, *Under the Canopy* (New York: George Braziller, 1982), p. 74.
29. Ibid., p. 66.
30. www.nobel.se/literature/laureates/1978/singer-lecture.html.
31. Zamir, *Journey to My Father*, p. 177.
32. Author's telephone interview with Robert Giroux, New York, April 29, 2002.
33. Author's interview with Dorotea Bromberg.
34. *Le Figaro*, December 11, 1976. This article was sent by Isaac Bashevis Singer's French publisher, Stock, to the Swedish Academy.
35. Author's telephone interview with Jean d'Ormesson, Paris, February 15, 2003.
36. In October 1978, Menachem Begin and Anwar Sadat, who had agreed to the Camp David Accords in September, were awarded the Nobel Peace Prize. In *Le Figaro*, October 6, 1978, Gérard Guillot characterized Singer's prize as entirely political. "In

1978," he writes, "everything in the world was done for Israel to agree to sign a durable peace with Egypt and the Arab countries. Honoring a writer who has always written in Yiddish was a way of maintaining that not only is Israel a nation, it is also a culture. It was also a way of giving support to the powerful Jewish lobby in the United States."

37. Edgar Reichmann, *Le Monde*, December 15, 1978.
38. Author's interview with Herbert Lottman.
39. Hadda, *Isaac Bashevis Singer*, p. 167.
40. Telushkin, *Master of Dreams*, p. 183.
41. Zamir, *Journey to My Father*, p. 93.
42. Author's interview with Israel Zamir, June 28, 2002.
43. Zamir, *Journey to My Father*, p. 91.
44. Lewi, *Isaac Bashevis Singer*, p. 41.

TEN. "THE GREATEST TRAGEDY WHICH COULD EVER HAPPEN TO A WRITER"

1. Telushkin, *Master of Dreams*, p. 267.
2. Ibid., p. 88.
3. Ibid.
4. Ibid., p. 101.
5. Ibid., p. 334.
6. *L'Arche*, August 1981.
7. Singer and Burgin, *Conversations*, p. 44.
8. Tuszynska, *Singer*, p. 275.
9. Singer and Burgin, *Conversations*, p. 67.
10. Ibid., p. 30.
11. Zamir, *Journey to My Father*, p. 221.
12. Singer and Burgin, *Conversations*, p. 94.
13. Ibid.
14. Ibid., p. 116.
15. Ibid., p. 178.
16. Ibid., p. 85.
17. Ibid., pp. 56–57.
18. Ibid., p. 135.
19. Ibid., p. 146.
20. Ibid., p. 58.
21. Farrell, *Isaac Bashevis Singer*, p. 101.
22. Ibid., p. 38.
23. Singer and Burgin, *Conversations*, p. 146.
24. Zamir, *Journey to My Father*, p. 226.
25. Author's conversation with Dvorah Telushkin.
26. Zamir, *Journey to My Father*, p. 213.
27. Ibid., p. 217.
28. Author's interview with Israel Zamir, June 29, 2002.
29. Zamir, *Journey to My Father*, p. 238.
30. Ibid., pp. 215, 216, 222.

31. Ibid., pp. 224–26.

32. Telushkin, *Master of Dreams*, pp. 314, 309.

33. Singer and Burgin, *Conversations*, p. 107.

34. Zamir, *Journey to My Father*, p. 203.

35. The engraving on the tombstone was subsequently corrected to read "Nobel Laureate" instead of "Noble Laureate."

36. Telushkin, *Master of Dreams*, p. 13.

37. Ibid.

38. This last novel was serialized in the *Forward* in 1956 and 1957, but only the first five chapters were translated into English, by Joseph Singer, Isaac's nephew. For some reason, it was never published in English. However, the second chapter, translated from the Yiddish by Joseph Sherman, is included in Seth L. Wolitz, ed., *The Hidden Isaac Bashevis Singer* (Austin: University of Texas Press, 2001), pp. 192–217.

39. Singer and Burgin, *Conversations*, p. 28.

40. Author's conversation with Kobi Weitzner, New York, April 30, 2002.

41. Author's conversation with Dorothea Straus.

42. Tuszynska, *Singer*, p. 385.

43. Singer and Burgin, *Conversations*, p. 161.

44. Singer, *A Young Man in Search of Love*, pp. 137, 139.

Selected Bibliography

WORKS BY ISAAC BASHEVIS SINGER

AUTOBIOGRAPHICAL WORKS

In My Father's Court. Translated by Channah Kleinerman-Goldstein, Elaine Gottlieb, and Joseph Singer. New York: Farrar, Straus and Giroux, 1966.

A Young Man in Search of Love. Garden City, NY: Doubleday, 1978.

Lost in America. Garden City, NY: Doubleday, 1981.

Isaac Bashevis Singer and Ira Moskowitz. *A Little Boy in Search of God: Mysticism in a Personal Light*. Garden City, NY: Doubleday, 1976.

Isaac Bashevis Singer and Richard Burgin. *Conversations with Isaac Bashevis Singer*. Garden City, NY: Doubleday, 1985.

More Stories from My Father's Court. Translated by Curt Leviant. New York: Farrar, Straus and Giroux, 2000.

NOVELS

The Family Moskat. Translated by A. H. Gross. New York: Alfred A. Knopf, 1950.

Satan in Goray. Translated by Jacob Sloan. New York: Noonday Press, 1955.

The Magician of Lublin. Translated by Elaine Gottlieb and Joseph Singer. New York: Noonday Press, 1960.

The Slave. Translated by Cecil Hemley. New York: Farrar, Straus and Giroux, 1962.

The Manor. Translated by Elaine Gottlieb and Joseph Singer. New York: Farrar, Straus and Giroux, 1967.

The Estate. Translated by Joseph Singer, Elaine Gottlieb, and Elizabeth Shub. New York: Farrar, Straus and Giroux, 1969.

Enemies, A Love Story. Translated by Aliza Shevrin and Elizabeth Shub. New York: Farrar, Straus and Giroux, 1972.

Shosha. Translated by Joseph Singer. New York: Farrar, Straus and Giroux, 1978.

The Penitent. New York: Farrar, Straus and Giroux, 1983.

The King of the Fields. New York: Farrar, Straus and Giroux, 1988.

Scum. Translated by Rosaline Dukalsky Schwartz. New York: Farrar, Straus and Giroux, 1991.

The Certificate. Translated by Leonard Wolf. New York: Farrar, Straus and Giroux, 1992.

Meshugah. Translated by Nili Wachtel. New York: Farrar, Straus and Giroux, 1994.

Shadows on the Hudson. Translated by Joseph Sherman. New York: Farrar, Straus and Giroux, 1998.

STORIES

The Spinoza of Market Street. New York: Farrar, Straus and Giroux, 1961.

Short Friday and Other Stories. New York: Farrar, Straus and Giroux, 1964.

The Seance and Other Stories. New York: Farrar, Straus and Giroux, 1968.

A Friend of Kafka and Other Stories. New York: Farrar, Straus and Giroux, 1970.

A Crown of Feathers and Other Stories. New York: Farrar, Straus and Giroux, 1973.

Passions and Other Stories. New York: Farrar, Straus and Giroux, 1975.

Old Love and Other Stories. New York: Farrar, Straus and Giroux, 1979.

The Image and Other Stories. New York: Farrar, Straus and Giroux, 1985.

The Death of Methuselah and Other Stories. New York: Farrar, Straus and Giroux, 1988.

Collected Stories. Edited by Ilan Stavans. 3 vols. New York: Library of America, 2004.

Gimpel the Fool and Other Stories. Translated by Saul Bellow. New York: Farrar, Straus and Giroux, 2006.

CHILDREN'S BOOKS

Zlateh the Goat and Other Stories. Translated by Elizabeth Shub. New York: Harper & Row, 1966.

The Fearsome Inn. Translated by Elizabeth Shub. New York: Scribner, 1967.

Mazel and Shlimazel, or The Milk of a Lioness. Translated by Elizabeth Shub. New York: Farrar, Straus and Giroux, 1967.

When Shlemiel Went to Warsaw and Other Stories. Translated by Elizabeth Shub. New York: Farrar, Straus and Giroux, 1968.

A Day of Pleasure: Stories of a Boy Growing Up in Warsaw. New York: Farrar, Straus and Giroux, 1969.

Elijah the Slave: A Hebrew Legend. Translated by Elizabeth Shub. New York: Farrar, Straus and Giroux, 1970.

Joseph and Koza, or The Sacrifice of the Vistula. Translated by Elizabeth Shub. New York: Farrar, Straus and Giroux, 1970.

Alone in the Wild Forest. Translated by Elizabeth Shub. New York: Farrar, Straus and Giroux, 1971.

The Topsy-Turvy Emperor of China. Translated by Elizabeth Shub. New York: Harper & Row, 1971.

The Wicked City. Translated by Elizabeth Shub. New York: Farrar, Straus and Giroux, 1972.

The Fools of Chelm and Their History. Translated by Elizabeth Shub. New York: Farrar, Straus and Giroux, 1973.

Why Noah Chose the Dove. Translated by Elizabeth Shub. New York: Farrar, Straus and Giroux, 1974.

A Tale of Three Wishes. New York: Farrar, Straus and Giroux, 1976.

Naftali the Storyteller and His Horse, Sus: and Other Stories. New York: Farrar, Straus and
    Giroux, 1976.
The Power of Light: Eight Stories for Hanukkah. New York: Farrar, Straus and Giroux,
    1980.
The Golem. New York: Farrar, Straus and Giroux, 1982.

WORKS ABOUT SINGER

Farrell, Grace, ed. *Isaac Bashevis Singer, Conversations*. Jackson: University Press of Missis-
    sippi, 1992.
Goran, Lester. *The Bright Streets of Surfside: The Memoir of a Friendship with Isaac Bashevis
    Singer*. Kent, OH: Kent State University Press, 1994.
Hadda, Janet. *Isaac Bashevis Singer*. New York: Oxford University Press, 1997.
Kresh, Paul. *Isaac Bashevis Singer: The Magician of West 86th Street*. New York: Dial Press,
    1979.
Straus, Dorothea. *Under the Canopy*. New York: George Braziller, 1982.
Telushkin, Dvorah. *Master of Dreams: A Memoir of Isaac Bashevis Singer*. New York:
    William Morrow, 1997.
Tuszynska, Agata. *Lost Landscapes: In Search of Isaac Bashevis Singer and the Jews of
    Poland*. Translated by Madeline G. Levine. New York: William Morrow, 1998.
Wolitz, Seth L., ed. *The Hidden Isaac Bashevis Singer*. Austin: University of Texas Press,
    2001.
Zamir, Israel. *Journey to My Father, Isaac Bashevis Singer*. Translated by Barbara Harshav.
    New York: Arcade Publishing, 1995.

FILMS

Davidson, Bruce. *Isaac Bashevis Singer's Nightmare and Mrs. Pupko's Beard*. 1971.
Hall, Richard, and Rabbi Daniel Syme. *Isaac Bashevis Singer, Champion of Yiddish Litera-
    ture*. 1985.
Mazursky, Paul. *Enemies, A Love Story*. 1989.
Nowak, Avram. *Isaac in America*. 1994.

Acknowledgments

~

I would like to thank all those who made this book possible by giving me their support and sharing their personal recollections, knowledge, and opinions.

My thanks to Isaac Bashevis Singer's family, particularly his son, Israel Zamir, and Israel's wife, Aviva, who shared their memories with me and gave me access to their personal archives.

My thanks to Dvorah Telushkin for trusting me and agreeing to answer my questions, and for welcoming me into her New York home in the company of her husband, Rabbi Joseph Telushkin.

My thanks to all of Isaac Bashevis Singer's friends, and especially the editors, translators, and agents who served his work so well: Roger Straus, Robert Giroux, André Bay, Dorotea Bromberg, Dorothea Straus, Marie-Pierre Bay, Herbert R. Lottman, and Michelle Lapautre. I owe a special thanks to Isaac Bashevis Singer's French translator, Marie-Pierre Bay, who helped and encouraged me throughout the writing of this book and whose valuable memories greatly facilitated my research.

My thanks to all those "keepers of memory," those who knew Singer personally and those who didn't, who helped me progress in my investigations: Michal Friedman, Agata Tuszynska, and Szulim Rozenberg for their descriptions of Jewish life in Poland before the Second World War and their memories of the ghetto and the Yiddish

Writers' Club. My thanks to Paul Morgensztern for entrusting me with his personal documents. My thanks to the American Jewish organizations devoted to preserving the memory and revival of Yiddish in Poland who received me in Warsaw.

My thanks to Bernard Osser and Alice Sedar, my translators and guides in Leoncin, Radzymin, Warsaw, and Krakow.

My thanks to the curators and librarians of the Bibliothèque Medem in Paris, as well as to all the Yiddishists who helped me with translations or research. Among them: Gilles Rozier; Isaac Niborski; Ariel Sion; Delphine Bechtel; Jacques Mandelbaum; Batia Baum; Charles Szlakmann; and Henri Lewi, a warm and unfailingly fascinating interlocutor, whose research on Singer and on Yiddish literature constantly guided me in this work. My thanks also to Rachel Ertel for her enlightening explanations concerning the Yiddish language and culture; to the editor Lydie Lachenal; and to Isy Morgensztern, whose stimulating opinions, as well as the excellent film on Isaac Bashevis Singer, helped me progress in my research.

My thanks to the curators and librarians of the Jewish Institute in Warsaw, the Musée d'Art et d'Histoire du Judaïsme in Paris, and the YIVO Institute for Jewish Research and Columbia University, both in New York. My thanks to the entire staff of the Harry Ransom Humanities Research Center in Austin, Texas, to its president, Thomas F. Staley, who allowed me to pursue my investigation, and to Seth L. Wolitz, chairman of Jewish studies at the University of Texas at Austin. My thanks also to Laurence Lévy, at the research department of *Le Monde*.

My thanks to the staff of the *Forward*, Kobi Weitzner, Lewis Katz, and Fanny Jacobson. My thanks as well to Leonard L. Milberg and Cynthia Ozick, who agreed to answer my questions, and to the American literature specialists Lazare Bitoun and Marc Saporta.

My thanks to the Nobel Foundation and to the members of the Nobel committee of the period, particularly Knut Ahnlund, who met me in Stockholm and gave me access to his personal papers.

My thanks to Jean-Marc Roberts and André Schiffrin for their faith in this venture. I would like to extend a special word of thanks to my friend Ellen Reeves for her precious advice.

My thanks, finally, to Betty Noiville and Martin Hirsch for their tireless readings, as well as to my three daughters, Raphaëlle, Mathilde, and Juliette, who bore this trial patiently while discovering *Zlateh the Goat* and *The Topsy-Turvy Emperor of China*.

Index